# GOVERNING EDUCATION

## Public Sector Reform or Privatization

### Paul C. Bauman

*School of Education*
*University of Colorado at Denver*

### Allyn and Bacon

Boston • London • Toronto • Sydney • Tokyo • Singapore

*Series Editor:* Ray Short
*Editorial Assistant:* Christine Shaw
*Marketing Manager:* Kathy Hunter
*Editorial-Production Administrator:* Donna Simons
*Editorial-Production Service:* Shepherd, Inc.
*Composition and Prepress Buyer:* Linda Cox
*Manufacturing Buyer:* Megan Cochran
*Cover Administrator:* Suzanne Harbison

Copyright © 1996 by Allyn & Bacon
A Simon & Schuster Company
Needham Heights, MA 02194

**Library of Congress Cataloging-in-Publication Data**

Bauman, Paul C.
    Governing education : public sector reform or privatization / Paul C. Bauman
      p.  cm.
    Includes bibliographical references and index.
    ISBN 0–205–16220–7
    1. School management and organization—United States.
  2. Educational change—United States.   3. Public schools—United States.
  4. Private schools—United States.  I. Title.
LB2805.B337  1996
371.2'00973—dc20                            95–35765
                                                          CIP

Printed in the United States of America

10  9  8  7  6  5  4  3  2  1      00  99  98  97  96  95

# CONTENTS

# PREFACE

Americans are facing a critical choice between two different systems of school control. We will either continue the current system of public governance or move to a privatized approach to schooling. Privatization, schools of choice, and charter schools are quickly gaining popularity and political support. These approaches to reform are designed to move away from or completely eliminate the authority of governing boards and local school districts. This more aggressive interest in governance reflects a major shift in emphasis from past school reforms directed at pedagogical issues and the quality of teaching. Governance reforms require changes in the balance of power in schools and communities and are consequently loaded with political controversy. Proposals emphasizing privatization and greater parental control reflect recent political trends in American society and a growing distrust of public institutions. The outcome of this decision—between a primarily public or private governance system—will have a significant impact on schools and the society at large, due to the size and scope of public education and the role of the schools in fostering democratic values.

I cannot think of three more contentious topics these days than politics, government, and the quality of public education. Yet polls show most Americans know very little about how public school systems are managed or governed. The purpose of this book is to help educators and citizens better understand the issues and opportunities associated with changes in educational governance. I have attempted to explain, demystify, and decipher the complexities inherent in the nation's largest public bureaucracy. At the same time, I have tried not to oversimplify a social system that will not be easy to change.

The first chapter describes a growing sense of uncertainty in public education and the problems within traditional approaches to educational governance. Chapter 2 focuses on different definitions of governance and governing in light of recent events in U.S. politics. Chapters 3 and 4 provide a brief overview of the historical and structural forces that define the governance environment in education. Controversies surrounding political and cultural values in a democratic society are highlighted in

Chapter 5. Chapter 6 summarizes school reforms that directly or indirectly impact the process of governance. Chapter 7 inventories critical skills for administrators and other participants in school and system-wide decision making. The future of educational governance is presented in Chapter 8 as a series of considerations for reforming the current system or moving to a privatized system of school control.

Readers will find four recurring themes throughout the book:

1. Reforming public education is a political matter, involving changes in priorities among core American values.
2. Democratic governance is inherently complex and controversial. Many of the reforms being considered are marked by contradiction and compromise among competing goals.
3. Dialogue is at the center of democratic governance. The quality and character of conversations between citizens, educators, and policymakers will influence the outcome of governance reform.
4. Changing the administration and control of public education is serious business. Children first learn about public institutions and the common good in schools.

The approach I have taken in this book is to weave together the best ideas and insights I could find from a variety of sources. The work of scholars, practitioners, advisory groups, and citizens comes together around the themes outlined above. The resulting diversity of ideas is a philosophical acknowledgment of the eclectic nature of a democratic society. My job was to search for convergence among different studies of educational governance without losing an appreciation for the diversity of viewpoints that exists.

This book is designed as a starting point for further investigation. Seminar questions and suggested readings are included to help the reader pursue this critical topic individually or through discussions with colleagues and community members. I hope these chapters encourage readers to seek out opportunities to participate in educational governance. We need to work together to improve public life, and the way we choose to govern schools is a good place to start.

Good ideas often come from the field of practice. This book evolved from a conversation about the design of a leadership program that would truly represent the political makeup of a community. I would like to thank Lou Weschler for his ideas about the four sectors of governance and his many insights about public organizations. Rex Brown, Ken Sirotnik, Roger Jackson, Mike Murphy, Ken Torp, and Allyn & Bacon's reviewers were instrumental in shaping this work. I appreciate the review of early drafts by Geoff Baumann, Ken Weaver, Patricia Chase, Jane Shellenberger, and the graduate students in my governance classes at the University of Colorado at Denver. I am indebted to Ray Short, Senior Editor at Allyn & Bacon, for both his encouragement and patience. Finally, this book would not have been written without the support of my wife Janet, daughter Erin, and my network of family and friends.

*Paul Bauman*
*Boulder, Colorado*
*January 1995*

# 1

# UNCERTAINTY IN PUBLIC EDUCATION

*Governing is far more important than government.*
—Haynes Johnson, journalist

Privatization, schools of choice, and site-based management are all attempts to change long held traditions of educational governance. After ten years of reform directed at teaching and learning, policy makers, educators, and citizens are asking more fundamental questions about who should control schools and how educational decisions should be made. These are political and organizational questions, and they are designed to bring about major changes in governance.

Increasing concern about the control of schools has come about in the last few years for several reasons. Governors and state legislators became more involved in school improvement in the 1980s with policy-driven approaches to raising standards, improving teaching, and requiring more rigorous curricula.[1] The involvement of high-level political figures helped attract new interest groups outside the traditional educational establishment, particularly the business community. These two powerful sectors of society soon discovered how difficult it would be to make fundamental changes in public education—the nation's largest civil bureaucracy. Political and business interests, along with educational researchers, consultants, academics, and citizens groups are in agreement that entirely new designs for sponsoring and controlling public education are necessary.

Interest in governance is demonstrated by the escalating number of research papers and journal articles.[2] The Institute for Educational

Leadership commented that three major reports urging governance reform were published between 1992 and 1993: "All of them are strong testimonials to the need for change."[3] Discussions about overhauling public education in the 1990s are focusing on privatizing public schools, increasing the use of home schooling, creating independent charter schools, and changing the management and control of public education in other essential ways. In many cities, school administrators are sensing that outright revolution against the traditional district system is on the minds of many Americans.

## POLITICAL AND SOCIAL CONCERNS

Focusing educational reform on issues of school control and management reflects broader concerns in the American political culture. Just as social and political movements in the past have influenced public education, political trends today help explain why governance is a hot topic in education. As Cohen states: "The politics of education is everywhere infused with, driven by, and even created by issues arising outside education. These issues change, sometimes with blinding speed. And since education in the U.S. is highly politicized, its political focus changes in response."[4]

Opinion polls and surveys report on Americans' cynicism and distrust of virtually all public agencies and programs. For example, the Center for Political Studies reported that the percentage of people who said they trust the U.S. Government "to do what is right most of the time" sunk to a thirty-year low of only 13 percent in 1993, compared to 62 percent in 1964.[5] Distrust appears to lead to cynicism and apathy as only 63 percent of U.S. households were willing to respond to the 1990 Census. Rates of income tax evasion rose to an all time-high in 1992. National, state, and local election results in 1992 and 1994 were characterized by many political observers as testimonials to the widespread frustration with government and to the prevailing desire for change.

Political scientists and pollsters continue to study the causes of the public's poor perception of government and the political process. Extensive research shows Americans have become increasingly skeptical about all large-scale organizations, public or private. The Kettering Foundation, reporting on the health of American democracy for over sixty years, observed that citizens increasingly think about public concerns in isolated and fragmented ways.[6] Many people feel disconnected from democratic politics, describing government as a national "problem," but irrelevant in their daily lives.

However, there is a parallel and seemingly contradictory view of American political values. The Kettering Foundation also notes that:

"Americans take great pride in having the world's oldest continuous democracy. They are proud of their political heritage—the extension of suffrage, the battles to protect individual rights, the ability to speak their minds. They identify with the values of a democratic order—freedom and justice."[7] These values have given rise to new and more direct forms of participation in government. Thomas Cronin[8] documents a nationwide movement from representative governance, through elected officials including state legislators and city council members, to the increasing use of voter referendums, ballot initiatives, constitutional amendments, and the recall of elected officials. Cronin calls this *direct democracy*, an idea that is taking shape in electronic town hall meetings, telephone surveys, and talk show politics. These changes suggest something profound is happening to traditional approaches to public participation.

Governing in the 1990s is clearly becoming more complex. Given a high level of access to information through computers and electronic networks, control and technical expertise is no longer limited to professional insiders. New groups are emerging that question or simply leave behind long-held governance structures. Cleveland points out that the notion of the public trust and the political process must be reconsidered:

> *In an information-rich polity, the very definition of control changes. Very large numbers of people empowered by knowledge—coming together in parties, unions, factions, lobbies, interest groups, neighborhoods, families, and hundreds of other structures—assert the right or feel the obligation to "make policy."*[9]

This is a profound challenge for the future of democractic governance. By definition, public organizations, particularly schools and public universities, are open systems, and are consequently not easy to control or organize. They are open to the public as consumers of services. They are also accessible by law to all taxpayers interested in how they are managed and financed. The results are evident in elementary and secondary schools. Teachers and administrators are aware of the need for community involvement. At the same time, they can be stifled by the multitude of interests present when decisions need to be made.

A constructive resolution to this paradox—between democratic and time consuming participation on the one hand, and the need for efficient, manageable systems on the other—is still an open question. And there are many who doubt that a democratic system can perform adequately in an increasingly diverse and polarized culture.[10] Whatever form American governance eventually takes, effective public decision making will always be critical in a democratic society. Despite anti-government ideologies and partisan political agendas, there is a constant need for public services that cannot or will not be provided by the private sector. However, just as Jefferson predicted, these systems are in need of constant renovation, hopefully by a well educated citizenry. The complexity of public problems—from health care to crime—will continually require improvements and advances in community governance. It seems that as the American culture changes, definitions of governance must change as well.

Public decision making has to take into account the diversity of racial, ethnic, and religious interests within communities. Although this challenge is sizable, it is not new. As Barry Bull points out: "From this country's inception, diversity has posed a practical and philosophical challenge to the very idea of a United States of America. . . . Thus, unity in diversity—or *e pluribus unum*, as it is expressed on the official seal of the United States—not only is possible but imposes on citizens a common moral obligation to provide for and to preserve one anothers' opportunities to choose and pursue their own visions of the good."[11]

History suggests that the alternative to effective, democratic governance is a decline in the quality of communities and more authoritarian forms of political decision making. Authoritarian governments not only prescribe the vision of the good life, but also the means by which it is achieved. Few people question therefore, that democratic governance must work. However, more and more policy makers and citizens are arguing about *how* it should work. The breadth and scope of these arguments suggest that traditional American governance systems will no longer be taken for granted, nor will they be entirely discarded.

## DEFINITION PROBLEMS

Observations of public and private organizations tend to produce complex and inconsistent definitions of the concept of governance. Educators and politicians are often operating with conflicting ideas of what governance is, much less what it should be. Many people do not recognize that they are attempting to change the decision-making process, and consequently the nature of governance itself.

Consider the different ways in which various stakeholders define governance. A state legislator or local school board member might argue that governance is defined with considerable legal specificity. Textbooks in educational administration and school law detail how the American political system delegates decision-making authority from the state level to local school boards in a decentralized system of state and local control. Representing state and local school boards, the 20th Century Fund published a report in which they define governance from a structural perspective:

> *America has chosen to govern its vast system of elementary and secondary education through a uniquely decentralized structure. More than fifteen thousand school boards are charged with responsibility for making the decisions that govern the education of millions of children in public schools across the country.*[12]

This report was presented in an effort to improve existing governance systems. After defining governance as a school board function, the report offers ways to improve school board legitimacy and performance, in essence strengthening and fine tuning the existing governance structure. This definition is technically accurate, but only reflects one dimension of governance. By definition governance reforms are limited to modifications in the existing structure.

*Politics, Markets, and America's Schools,* Chubb and Moe's popular and controversial book, challenged this definition by taking a critical look at the traditional governance structure in American education.

> *Today, this system is so thoroughly taken for granted that it virtually defines what Americans mean by democratic governance of the public schools. At its heart are the school district and its institutions of democratic control: the school board, the superintendent, and the district office. The school board is the district's legislative body and is almost always elected. The superintendent is its administrative head and is sometimes elected, sometimes appointed. The district office is the bureaucratic organization responsible for carrying out the policies of the board and the superintendent. . . . This system of governance has been firmly in place now for as long as most Americans can remember.*[13]

The authors create considerable controversy with the remainder of the book's observations that this system is not working and is largely responsible for the problems of public education: "For reasons we will elaborate and document at length, the specific kinds of democratic institutions by which American public education has been governed for the last half century appear to be incompatible with effective schooling."[14] The tone of their review of traditional governance as the foundation of a bureaucratic and politically exclusive system signals to the reader that they believe that there is a lot more to governance than local control.

Defining governance in bureaucratic terms creates a serious conflict of values for educational administrators. Efforts to improve schooling have long emphasized rational management techniques and bureaucratic principles applied to large organizations. Administrators were trained to manage comprehensive schools that had been organized to serve large numbers of students. They were equipped to direct a staff of specialists through the implementation of scientific-legalistic norms.[15] For reformers to conclude suddenly that the root of the problem is this bureaucratic structure questions not only the administrative process, but also the abilities and orientations of the administrators themselves. In a positive sense, bureaucratic administration is associated with the values of efficiency and effectiveness; but in today's' anti-institutional climate, bureaucracy is viewed as synonymous with waste and inflexibility. As a consequence of these opposing views, administrators must think carefully about how they are defining educational governance and constructing improvements.

It is difficult to determine how students, parents, and other community members define educational governance. Many people believe that teachers and school administrators set policy and *are unaware* of the school district system, governed by democratically elected school boards. Parents are often unaware that school boards and school districts are independent government agencies, separate from city and county government. Many people believe that educational governance is simply a matter of local control and dismiss the need to question a long held tradition. Yet the complexity and sheer dimensions of public education in the U.S. suggest local governance may be a myth. Local boards do not control the manufacture of textbooks that their students use. They do not govern teacher preparation or certification. They do not govern the exams that measure math and reading, or those that will determine or prohibit university admissions. School boards cannot completely govern the architecture of their school buildings.[16] Public schools are now controlled by a much more complex, overlapping system of institutions and decision makers. Organizational forces in the nation's largest public enterprise do not just come from locally elected boards of education.

When these differing views of educational governance are added to the diversity of ideas about what governance *should be*, it is easy to see why the public schools' system for making decisions often seems more complicated and inaccessible than that of other public or private organizations. Governance includes legal systems for making authoritative decisions, but it also includes the multiple actors and interest groups involved in schooling. Governors, administrators, teachers, parents, students, and reformers are governing when they become active in making important decisions about how schools operate. If educational leaders are going to succeed in this environment and involve the public in the process, they will need a good understanding of formal governance structures as well as the informal and often complex qualities of governance as political dialogue. Thus, because this process is a critical part of a democratic society, educational administrators are in powerful positions either to support or to inhibit representative methods of educational decision making.

## COMPLEX GOALS

Examining the basic purpose of public education is a logical way of identifying problems in the system and generating solutions. A clear statement of purpose usually forms the basis of measurable goals, operational procedures, staff functions, and evaluation systems in a rationally designed organization. Purpose defines the way an organization will be envisioned, clarifies its reason for being, and shapes the behaviors and values of its members.[17]

Public education, however, is not designed exclusively on formal and rational organizational principles. The goals of public education have been debated, restated, and reorganized throughout American history. Schools are repeatedly called upon to affect large changes in society, from the creation of a common culture in the 19th Century, to preparing graduates to compete with foreign nations in science and technology in the 1950s, to helping students access the information highway in the 1990s. The goals of the public schools are further complicated by the decentralized structure of the American system, which allows each state and thousands of local school districts to interpret and tailor school systems to meet local needs. Because of the complexity of goals, unclear technologies, and fluid participation by many groups, schools have been described as "organized anarchies."[18]

There are, however, two very broad and generally accepted purposes for public education; the development of the individual and the promotion of the general welfare of society. These can be described as the private and social purposes of schools.[19] Some of the dilemmas brought about by the complexity of goals in American education follow.

### Education and the Individual

It has long been established that schooling benefits the individual in countless ways. Recent studies of the information economy and related employment skills show a clear link between education and personal earnings.[20] Educated persons are likely to be employed at more interesting and higher paid jobs than are less educated individuals. Schooling opens up the possibility of more schooling, which leads to better employment possibilities. With greater resources at their disposal, more educated individuals are likely to have more options for the use of leisure time. As more informed consumers, recipients of education are more likely to get more for their resources and are likely to enjoy a better diet and have better health practices.[21] Education is also a source of inspiration, personal development, well-being in adulthood, and a variety of other complex, private benefits.

The development of the individual as a participant in the public schools is a complex process. Volumes of research document and categorize multitudes of factors that influence an individual in the course of schooling. One stream of research details the importance of internal, organizational characteristics, such as social relations among students and teachers, and the culture of the school as a work place.[22] Another set of research documents the importance of the external characteristics of schools, such as parental involvement, student body composition, and school size.[23] Although there is considerable disagreement in the research and policy making communities about which factors are most important, and which ones are the keys to reform, there is general agreement that the individual is influenced by the organization and design of schooling.

Governance systems are an integral part of the organization of schools. They are required for making practical, day-to-day decisions about the internal and external factors that affect teaching and learning. Governance systems are established to mediate between different philosophical views of effective education. Students as individual learners are the direct recipients of governance decisions including what subjects they are to study. Students are also indirectly influenced by the symbolic quality of the schools' governance system. The schools are the place where young people see and feel the results of shared beliefs and social values. They are the recipients and observers of either effective or ineffective educational governance.

## Education and Society

The second broad goal of public education is to promote the general welfare of society. By enhancing the qualities of the individual, education benefits the community. Additionally, society is able to promote social values through the schools in what Dewey described as intentional and formal ways. Democracies rely on the schools to provide individuals with common civic values and knowledge required to support the political, social, and economic institutions that comprise those societies.[24]

The way schools are governed is an overt or indirect statement about how a community interprets and promotes the general welfare and how it believes democracy should work. In essence, governing is both part of the educational experience and reliant upon its success. Jefferson stressed the importance of an educated citizenry for the future of American democracy, and the two systems have been closely connected ever since: "I know no safe depository of the ultimate powers of the society but the people themselves; and if we think them not enlightened enough to exercise their control with a wholesome discretion, the remedy is not to take it from them, but to inform their discretion by education."[25]

The interplay between education, the individual, and society creates a complex set of political relationships. The creation of an educational system that is both free and compulsory highlights the degree to which Americans believe in the schools as a mechanism to support the economy and the community. Economic productivity is linked to education through human capital development—the principle that education increases the skill and capacity of workers. Community-building or civic purposes of education relate to benefits that affect personal, family, and political life. However, there is a continuous tension between the economic and civic purposes of education. Resources used to enhance personal sensibilities may or may not lead to greater productivity, and economically valuable knowledge and skills may or may not enhance personal, family, or community life.[26] When an educational system is designed around these kinds of broad purposes and complex goals, it is understandable that governance is so challenging.

For better or worse, educational governance is an example of America's decentralized system of political democracy in every community. Practically, it is the political system that controls learning environments; and the political environment of a school plays a key role in preparing young Americans to participate in governance as adults. Barry Bull states: "Our attitudes toward schools are closely related to our vision of the moral purpose of government. After all, how public schools—which are agencies of the state—are to treat our youngest citizens and what they may legitimately expect our children to become as adults logically depends on our beliefs about the moral authority and responsibilities of government."[27]

The close relationship between the schools and the general welfare of society was captured in the report *A Nation at Risk* by the National Commission on Excellence in Education, which is widely credited with initiating many school reforms in the 1980s.[28] The tenor of the report was one of alarm and crisis. The connection between a healthy educational system and a healthy society was the premise for the entire report. Observers across the country agreed that there was a serious problem in education. In 1982, Weiler stated: "the phenomenon of declining confidence in both education and the state, and the apparent interaction between the two, have developed to a point where they should become a matter of serious concern to those who educate and those who are being educated, as well as to those who rule and to those who are being ruled in this country."[29] Concern about the quality of the public schools continues, both on the grounds of economic productivity and community health.

## Measuring Educational Outcomes

If there is agreement over the importance of education as a societal value, it is based on abstract statements about an activity designed to promote learning and the acquisition and dissemination of knowledge. It is assumed that knowledge is gained by individuals in the process of experiencing an education. However, learning is a highly individualistic phenomenon. The public schools have attempted to support multiple ways of learning and disseminating knowledge. Schools deal with abstract links between information, skills, wisdom, and understanding. The body of knowledge that is created and distributed is affected by a combination of interrelated social and political factors present within schools. The degree and rate of which knowledge is attained is determined to some degree by the individual, but also by teachers, and the quality of the learning environment.

It is difficult to measure the attainment of goals under these conditions. The social nature of schooling thwarts the application of scientific approaches that rely on objective determinations of inputs and outputs. How can a system measure when a person is *educated* or *knowledgeable*, much less how the process occurred? Schools are inevitably faced with difficult measurement problems. The challenge of accurately and efficiently measuring outcomes has persisted in the schools for decades. How to assess student performance is the basis of wide differences in teaching methods, curricular designs, and approaches to system-wide reform. Countless research studies have attempted to isolate variables that impact learning. "Probably no other public-sector endeavor is characterized by as much record keeping, measurement, and assessment as public schooling. . . . However, simply because educational measurement occurs on a broad scale does not mean that the efforts are accurate, understandable, or useful."[30]

Measurement issues are intensifying in the 1990s. The educational community is highly divided over "outcome-based" education, in which changes in teaching and learning are driven by the identification of outcomes. Clear statements of skills and desired competencies as outcomes of schooling will in theory lead to more focused teaching and practical learning. However, schools are not alone in affecting educational outcomes. Because a person learns while he or she is involved in schooling does not mean schooling is responsible for learning. As Dewey pointed out long ago, students learn a great deal from the environment outside of the school setting. Schools promote learning but are only a small part of the learning process. Dewey described *incidental* learning as the education everyone gets simply from living with others. Learning in schools, however, is *intentional*. The family, religion, and work provide knowledge in an incidental way. Schools, on the other hand, are intentional social agencies, an important means for transmitting culture. Dewey argued that schools are only one among many ways of transmitting culture and knowledge, and when compared with other agencies, such as the family, a relatively superficial means.[31] Consequently, attempts to rationally or logically measure the outcomes of schooling are more challenging than most other public or private sector activities. Measurement questions are at the center of many governance debates.

## Education in the Information Age

Advances in information-related technologies and the growth of an information-based economy are raising important questions about the purpose of public education. If one of the purposes of the schools is to provide students with skills necessary to participate in the economy, schools must change to meet the needs of a post-industrial, knowledge-based economy. The expansion of knowledge-work is transforming the technical skills and social requirements of the labor force. Necessary skills include working with abstract symbols, creative thinking and problem solving, ability to work in cooperative groups, and developing a sense of complex systems. Keedy states: "A major societal shift requires adoption of new goals and instructional strategies for schooling. Ultimately, this 'domain shift' means different organizational structures and relationships in schools because the structure of school organizations has not kept up the technical and social requirements for the work force."[32] Teaching methods must shift to help students learn new skills in new ways. Administrative practices need to take into account different approaches to scheduling, facility usage, and private sector involvement in instructional delivery.

The information-based economy has important implications for public policies designed to achieve equal educational opportunities. Information is different from other kinds of physical resources that can be controlled and allocated in ways that promote equity and fairness. Information is neither scarce nor finite, and its dissemination and use is difficult if not impossible to control. Access becomes a critical issue for educators. Federal, state, and local government agencies, and communications industries are trying to determine how information can be made available to the public outside of the private marketplace. Access to cable television, computer networks, and the "information highway" are now important resources for schools and the electorate in a democracy.

These different conceptions of the purposes of public education create problems for reformers and educators. Causal relationships between reforms and changes in student performance are difficult to measure. Many of the technical solutions for organizational problems borrowed from private industry are ineffective in the complex social environment of the public schools.

## GOVERNANCE AND EDUCATIONAL LEADERSHIP

The interaction and interdependence between public education and a democratic form of government has created a contentious yet critical role for those involved in educational governance. Governance involves politics. It requires interpersonal skills and character, as well as the ability to analyze and effectively deal with complex public organizations. Educational leaders must be sensitive to changing conditions in schools and in society. They also must be alert to the motives behind educational reforms that are focusing more on the sponsorship, management, and control of schooling. Many of the proposed governance changes in the 1990s are directed at the system of elected leadership on state and local school boards as well as appointed leadership in school districts, buildings, and classrooms.

In order to operate effectively in the politicized environment of the 1990s, educational leaders will need to face the complex nature of governance. They will need a broad set of leadership abilities required in socially diverse, public settings. As school reform takes on more complex qualities—from outcome-based education to new school finance systems—administrators will be required to rethink governance systems that fully support school improvement. State policy makers and building administrators are being called upon to change the perceived and/or real isolation of school districts. Usdan observed: "The reality is that public education will have to build much broader political coalitions with other groups. Schools must break out of their provincialism and recognize the political reality of these new constituencies and work with them."[33] Site-based management, institutional choice, school-linked children services, and alternative funding for schools all require an ability to work with outside interests and to think differently about the process of governing.

### Changing Educational Governance

In a reactive sense, this book describes changes in educational governance that are taking place as a result of the school reforms and political trends that started in the last twenty-five years. Proposed governance changes in the 1990s, including schools of choice, charter schools, and site-based management, represent diverse political and ideological interests in public education. This book will consider the relationship between societies' values and attitudes about the public sector, democratic governance, and school reform.

This book is also about changing educational governance from a proactive standpoint. As long as public schools exist, administrators, policy makers, teachers, and educators in other positions will need democratic forms of decision making and community involvement. Changes in traditional governance structures that meet the demands of a more active and informed citizenry will be required; but changes in traditions and organizations are not easy to achieve. Public education is a complex system of competing values and numerous special interests. Any major changes in governance must recognize that the present system was designed to reflect the values of representative democracy, through elected school boards and public school districts. Governance is about civic values, and will require patience and openness. Changes must be generated from more than empirical evidence of low voting patterns in school board elections or scientific studies of administrative efficiency. Changing political systems will require a sensitivity to a complex balance of values, opinions, and beliefs of individuals, communities, and organizations. At the same time, improvements in educational governance must include the public's changing views of democratic action and how they are linked to practical concerns.

This book relies on an approach to information and knowledge that takes into account the nonscientific, political nature of governing. Sirotnik's description of *critical inquiry* provides a useful framework for understanding a complex topic that has moral, philosophical, and practical dimensions.[34] Sirotnik states: "Knowledge generated in human action has purpose, and with purpose come values and human interests. There is little to be gained, therefore, in the expectation that knowledge will be utilized without the concomitant expectation that values and human interests need to be explicit in the knowledge-generating process."[35] This approach emphasizes that in order to make practical use of research and theory, the user of that knowledge must think *critically*, and consider the values and attitudes that he or she brings to understanding and using that knowledge. In other words, readers are asked to think critically about educational governance, and examine their personal and political values as they endorse or discard reforms such as privatization.

A *critical* approach uses a series of generic questions "oriented toward developing a working consensus and agendas for action."[36] Using this approach, this book is designed to provide opportunities and insights for eventual practical action, based on the widely held American value of democratic control and open participation in public institutions. These generic questions provide a structure and sequence for the reader.

### Question 1: What Are We Doing Now, and How Did It Come to Be This Way?

First, participants in educational governance must remember that the problems they are facing have a current and historical context, both of which must be considered. The first section of the book deals with the history and structure of traditional educational governance to provide the background for contemporary debates and reforms.

### Question 2: Who's Interests Are and Are Not Being Served by the Way Things Are?

To support a truly *critical* understanding of educational governance, the middle section of the book examines the political dimensions of governance, including administration, policy making, changing demographics, and nationwide school reforms.

### Question 3: What Information and Knowledge Do We Have, or Need to Get, That Bear Upon the Issues?

This question is directed at the many informal aspects of governance that are frequently overlooked. Many reformers and citizens groups believe that traditional structures are *the* problem and should be the focus of attention. But the changing characteristics, qualities, and cultures of school systems and educators themselves must also be considered. Chapters 4 and 5 include information from many sources about these sometimes subtle aspects of governing. One example is the increasing involvement of public and private agencies in schools through partnerships and cooperative agreements. Linkages between schools and outside organizations influence governance patterns in ways that are often indirect and not addressed as governance-related.

### Question 4: Is This the Way We Want Things to Be, and What Are We Going to Do about All This?

Finally, educational leaders must remember that all is not talk and study, that actions can and must be taken, reviewed, revised, and reconsidered. Governance reforms reviewed in Chapter 6 demonstrate that many Americans don't want things to continue as they are. The last two chapters of the book focus on the critical question of improving educational governance. Chapter 7 considers the skills educational leaders will need to achieve thoughtful and informed changes in governance in light of predicted changes in communities across the United States.

## Practicing Governance

Governance frequently involves discussion, debate and dialogue. Prospective school administrators, policy makers, and parents need opportunities to practice the complex art of political discourse in informal and educational settings. Seminar questions are included at the end of each chapter to initiate conversations that involve complex political considerations. Good seminars are not designed to produce right or wrong answers or definitive solutions to problems. They offer participants the opportunity to practice and develop the sometimes subtle skills of politics, persuasion, and power outlined in Chapter 7. Socratic seminars are structured to promote an enhanced understanding of values and attitudes. Readers interested in sponsoring lively and challenging discussions are urged to incorporate many of the seminar ground rules outlined by Mortimer Adler in the *Paideia Program*. Sirotnik and Oakes' characterization of critical inquiry and critical dialogue in *Critical Perspectives on the Organization and Improvement of Schooling*[38] is also a helpful guide to serious discussion. Additionally, each chapter includes a brief list of suggested readings about some of the most important educational and political issues of our times.

## SUMMARY

Fundamental changes in educational governance are central to school reform in the 1990s. Market-driven schools of choice and site-based decision making are direct attempts to change long-held traditions of educational governance. Political trends help explain why governance is a hot topic in education, just as other social and political movements have influenced public education in the past.

Whatever form educational governance eventually takes, effective public decision making will always be essential for a democratic society. The ways in which the public schools are controlled and managed are important for individual students as well as the society at large. Democratic governance is required for broad policy making as well as for practical, day-to-day decisions about the internal and external factors that affect teaching and learning.

In order to operate effectively in the politicized environment of the 1990s, educational leaders will need to face the complex nature of governance—the system for controlling and influencing public schools. When differing definitions of educational governance are added to the diversity of ideas about what governance *should be*, it is easy to see why education's system for making decisions often seems more complicated and inaccessible than other public or private organizations. If educational leaders are going to improve this environment, and involve the public in the schools, they will need a good understanding of the school district system as well as the often complex qualities of governance as a political dialogue.

Changing political systems will require a sensitivity to the complex mix of values, opinions, and beliefs of individuals, communities, and organizations. Improvements in educational governance must consider the public's changing views of democratic participation and practical action.

## SEMINAR QUESTIONS

1. Do you believe that people in your community are apathetic and cynical about government and politics? If you think they are, what are the consequences for public education?

2. Do you think school-level governance affects teaching and learning? If so, how?

3. Do you believe proposed reforms of educational governance, such as site-based management and schools of choice, will support the values of democratic governance?

## SUGGESTED READINGS

Cronin, Thomas. *Direct Democracy: The Politics of Initiatives, Referendum, and Recall.* Cambridge: Harvard University Press, 1989.

Danzberger, Jacqueline P., Michael W. Kirst, and Michael D. Usdan. *Governing Public Schools: New Times New Requirements.* Washington, DC: Institute for Educational Leadership, 1992.

The Kettering Foundation. *Meaningful Chaos: How People Form Relationships with Public Concerns.* Dayton, Ohio, 1993.

Sirotnik, Kenneth and Jeannie Oakes. *Critical Perspectives on the Organization and Improvement of Schooling.* Boston: Kluwer-Nijhoff, 1986.

Yankelovich, Daniel. *Coming to Public Judgment.* Syracuse, New York: Syracuse University Press, 1991.

## ENDNOTES

1. Michael W. Kirst, "Who Would Control the Schools? Reassessing Current Policies," in *Schooling for Tomorrow: Directing Reforms to Issues That Count*, ed. Thomas J. Sergiovanni and John H. Moore (Boston: Allyn and Bacon, 1989), pp. 62–87.

2. "Researchers Delve into Governance Issues," *The School Administrator* February, 1993, pp. 34–35. This publication reported in 1993 that there was a 10% annual increase in research papers on governance topics submitted to the American Educational Research Association.

3. Jacqueline P. Danzberger, Michael W. Kirst, and Michael D. Usdan, *Governing Public Schools: New Times New Requirements* (Washington, D.C.: Institute for Educational Leadership, 1992), p. XII.
4. David K. Cohen, "Governance and Instruction: The Promise of Decentralization," in *Choice and Control in American Education*, vol. 1, eds. William H. Clune and John F. Witte (New York: Falmer, 1990), p. 364.
5. The Center for Political Studies, University of Michigan (1964–1992); Los Angeles Times Poll (1993), "America the Cynical," *Time*, July 19, 1993, p. 17.
6. The Kettering Foundation, *Meaningful Chaos: How People Form Relationships with Public Concerns* (Dayton, Ohio, 1993). Also see The Kettering Foundation, *Citizens and Politics: A View from Main Street America* (Dayton, Ohio, 1991) and Mary Anne Raywid, "Rethinking School Governance," in *Restructuring Schools: The Next Generation of Educational Reform* (San Francisco: Jossey-Bass, Inc. 1990), pp. 152–203.
7. The Kettering Foundation, *Citizens and Politics: A View from Main Street America* (Dayton, Ohio, 1991), p. iv.
8. Thomas Cronin, *Direct Democracy: The Politics of Initiatives, Referendum, and Recall* (Cambridge: Harvard University Press, 1989).
9. Harlan Cleveland, "The Twilight of Hierarchy," *Kettering Review* Summer 1993, p. 49.
10. Christopher Lasch, *The True and Only Heaven: Progress and Its Critics* (New York: W.W. Norton & Co., 1991). Also see Arthur M. Schlesinger, Jr., *The Disuniting of America: Reflections on a Multicultural Society* (New York: W.W. Norton & Co., 1992), and John Rawls, *Political Liberalism* (New York: Columbia University Press, 1993).
11. Barry L. Bull, "The Limits of Teacher Professionalization," in *The Moral Dimensions of Teaching*, ed. John I. Goodlad, Roger Soder, and Kenneth A. Sirotnik (San Francisco: Jossey-Bass, Inc., 1990), pp. 87–129.
12. National School Boards Association, "Report of the Twentieth Century Fund Task Force on School Governance." New York: The Twentieth Century Fund Press. 1992. p. Foreword.
13. John E. Chubb and Terry M. Moe, *Politics, Markets, and America's Schools* (Washington, DC: Brookings, 1991), p. 5.
14. Chubb and Moe, *Politics, Markets, and America's Schools*, p. 2.
15. Anthony S. Bryk, Valerie E. Lee and Julia B. Smith, "High School Organization and Its Effect on Teachers and Students: An Interpretive Summary of the Research," in *Choice and Control in American Education*, vol. 1, ed. William H. Clune and John F. Witte (New York: Falmer, 1990), pp. 137–138.
16. Jonothon Kozol, *Savage Inequalities* (New York: Crown Publishers, 1991), p. 212.
17. Phillip C. Schlechty, *Schools for the Twenty-First Century: Leadership Imperatives for Educational Reform* (San Francisco: Jossey-Bass, 1990), p. 3.
18. Michael D. Cohen and James G. March, *Leadership and Ambiguity* (Boston: Harvard Business School Press, 1986), p. 3.
19. Henry M. Levin, "The Theory of Choice Applied to Education," in *Choice and Control in American Education*, vol. 1, ed. W.H. Clune & J.F. Witte (New York: Falmer, 1990), pp. 247–284. Also see Cora B. Marrett, "School Organization and the Quest for Community," in *Choice and Control in American Education*, vol. 1, eds. William H. Clune and John F. Witte (New York: Falmer, 1990), pp. 235–246.

20. James G. Ward, "Analysis of Demographic Change, Cultural Diversity and School Finance Policy," in *The New Politics of Race and Gender*, Catherine Marshall, ed. (Washington, DC: Falmer Press 1993). p. 11. Ward cites Robert Reich, *The Work of Nations: Preparing Ourselves for 21st Century Capitalism* (New York: Knopf, 1991).
21. Austin D. Swanson and Richard A. King, *School Finance: Its Economics and Politics*, (New York: Longman, 1991), p. 4.
22. Bryk, *Choice and Control in American Education*, vol. 1, pp. 135–226.
23. Bryk, *Choice and Control in American Education*, vol. 1, pp. 135–226.
24. Levin, *Choice and Control in American Education*, vol. 1, p. 251.
25. Robert J. Honeywell, *The Educational Work of Thomas Jefferson* (Cambridge, Mass.: Harvard University Press, 1931).
26. Douglas E. Mitchell, "Education Politics for the New Century: Past Issues and Future Directions," in *Education Politics for the New Century* (Washington, DC: Falmer Press, 1990), p. 161.
27. Barry L. Bull, "The Limits of Teacher Professionalization," in *The Moral Dimensions of Teaching*, ed. John I. Goodlad, Roger Soder, and Kenneth A. Sirotnik (San Francisco: Jossey-Bass, 1990), p. 88.
28. National Commission on Excellence in Education, *A Nation at Risk: The Imperative for Educational Reform*, (Washington, DC.: U.S. Government Printing Office, 1983).
29. Hans N. Weiler, *Education, Public Confidence, and the Legitimacy of the Modern State: Is There a "Crisis" Somewhere?* Institute for Research on Educational Finance and Governance, Program Report No. 82-B4. (Stanford University, June, 1982), p. 1.
30. James W. Guthrie, "Investing Education Dollars: Do We Need a 'Dow Jones Index' for America's Schools," in *Rethinking School Finance: An Agenda for the 1990s* ed. Allen R. Odden (San Francisco: Jossey-Bass, 1992), pp. 202–203.
31. Lawrence A. Cremin, "Public Education and the Education of the Public," in *History, Education, and Public Policy*, ed. Donald R. Warren (Berkeley, Calif.: McCutchan Publishing Corporation, 1978), pp. 30–31.
32. John L. Keedy, "The Twin Engines of School Reform for the 1990s: The School Sites and National Coalitions," *Journal of School Leadership* 4, No. 1 (January 1994): 94–111.
33. Michael Usdan, "Emerging Leadership Needs in Education," *National Civic Review* 80, (1991): 49.
34. Kenneth Sirotnik and Jeannie Oakes, *Critical Perspectives on the Organization and Improvement of Schooling* (Boston: Kluwer-Nijhoff, 1986).
35. Kenneth A. Sirotnik, "The School as the Center of Change," in *Schooling for Tomorrow: Directing Reforms to Issues That Count*, ed. Thomas J. Sergiovanni & John H. Moore (Boston: Allyn and Bacon, 1989), p. 97.
36. Sirotnik, "The School as the Center of Change," p. 99.
37. Mortimer J. Adler, *The Paideia Program: An Educational Syllabus* (New York: Collier Books, 1984).
38. Kenneth Sirotnik and Jeannie Oakes, *Critical Perspectives on the Organization and Improvement of Schooling* (Boston: Kluwer-Nijhoff, 1986).

# 2

## DEFINITIONS AND INTERPRETATIONS OF GOVERNANCE

*Never doubt that a small group of dedicated citizens can change the world. Indeed it is the only thing that ever has.*
—Margaret Mead

*Governance* refers to formal systems as well as informal procedures for controlling and managing people and organizations. In education, governance is about running schools and deciding how, when, and where they will operate.

Formally, governance is the exercise of public authority to achieve common goals as determined by a democratic majority. The American political system limits and theoretically balances power between three branches of government in a federalist system of national, state, and local jurisdictions. Elected and appointed officials are designated as policy makers and governors of agencies, personnel, and programs.

American governance involves the actions of countless individuals and organizations. By design, governance systems and their participants reflect differences in community values. Public policies are the result of compromises between competing interests and ideologies. The U.S. Constitution established a system designed to promote the general welfare, protect individual rights, and assure freedom from undue government intervention in the protection of those rights. Policy makers are consequently challenged to reconcile competing and apparently contradictory values. The complexity of the American system emerges from programs and policies that are supposed to be both equitable and efficient, and supportive of both individual liberty and the security of the community. Complexity arises in a system that is both decentralized, through state and local jurisdictions, and centralized through federal agencies and nationwide policies and programs.

Informally, governance is a dynamic process, open to the vagaries of interpersonal power and persuasion. Governance can take shape in a conversation when an administrator or citizen exerts influence. Politics is not restricted to formal settings, such as city council meetings or in the halls of state legislatures. Governing is an active process that occurs when people discuss the design and control of public institutions. In public education, governance is not just what school boards do. It is a bigger and more inclusive activity, whether participants know it or not. Governance in action is unpredictable, occasionally arbitrary, and irrational. Governance involves politics and questions of who gets what, when, and how.[1]

The American system of governance is being defined from many different points of view. Each definition seems to influence the way power is distributed. The following descriptions of formal and informal governance demonstrate the complexity and controversy surrounding educational politics in the 1990s.

## STRUCTURAL-BUREAUCRATIC DEFINITIONS

Governance is generally defined in public sector organizations in formal, bureaucratic terms. Government institutions operate with legal authority to provide services, allocate resources, and regulate the behavior of individuals and businesses on behalf of the public interest. Governing bodies formulate and implement policies within legal constraints established to protect citizens' rights.[2] If a community member wants to participate in the decision making process, he or she can register to vote, run for elected office, or seek an appointment in a public agency. Studies of citizen participation in government show a majority of Americans view governance in formal, bureaucratic terms.

Progressive reforms in the first half of the twentieth century bureaucratized the governance of public agencies to eliminate the problems of political favoritism and corruption. Scientific management strengthened bureaucratic structures and professionalized government employment. The effects of these reforms are still in place today. The structural view of governance emphasizes efficiency, rationally-designed organizational charts, and formal agreements between agencies and levels of government. Laws and regulations determine how authority is allocated from federal to local jurisdictions. Federal and state constitutions establish executive, legislative, and judicial functions at each level of policy implementation.

Studies of governance reform from a structural-bureaucratic standpoint focus on shifts in formal political authority between levels of government. For example, the Reagan Presidency promoted *New Federalism* and the devolution of government. Responsibilities for decision making were shifted away from federal agencies to lower levels of governing authority.[3] In educational governance, state-level authority increased during this period.

The problem with defining governance from a formal and structural perspective is that it delimits and allocates power and authority only to existing institutions and administrative positions. Government is viewed in bureaucratic terms, as something abstract and separate from the community. Governing is associated with a legalistic, political process. With this definition alone, citizens think of public authority as the sole domain of federal, state, and local agencies and the business of a few officials.[4] The exclusionary quality of a structural definition for governance is often overlooked. Governance is people in communities, not the government, and some distant decision-making elites.[5] Either overtly or covertly, the structural approach determines who governs, and consequently, who doesn't. Bureaucracies become exclusionary and limiting by definition. Governmental structures are certainly part of governance, but not the sole arbiter of public concerns.

## CONTEXTUAL DEFINITIONS

Governance is often defined within a specific and narrow context. Contextual definitions also control participation and modify the meaning of governance in order to pursue certain ends. For example, teachers and teacher educators can define governance in ways that better represent their interests and issues. Classroom teachers identify themselves as critical players in decision making by virtue of their central roles in school systems—systems designed around teaching and learning. Research on the implementation of state-wide curriculum changes and other top down reforms demonstrates the power of teachers in decision making and governance. Classroom teachers cannot be considered neutral agents, and devoid of any governance responsibilities or powers. Although policy makers and reformers may not accept it, teachers play a critical role in educational governance, particularly through their positions as implementers and shapers of state and district policies.

If 2.2 million classroom teachers influence the governance process, it is important to consider who influences their approach to governance and prepares them to perform effectively within a political and value-laden environment. The following depiction of three modes of governing teacher preparation demonstrates the influence of context on decision making:

1. Political modes—The dominant mode in American teacher preparation, in which elected state boards of education and state legislatures are the principal arenas of expression and influence.
2. Institutional modes—Schools, colleges, and departments of education prepare teachers and consequently exercise considerable latitude in designing and implementing preparation programs.
3. Professional modes—Representing the fullest expression for profession-based expertise and values, three different examples of preparation and control exist: states with independent professional standards and practices boards for governing teacher education; the national voluntary accreditation mechanism (NCATE); and third, the National Board for Professional Teaching Standards Board (NBPTS), a newly developing organization.[7]

Each of these modes view governance in practical and constructive ways; but they differ significantly in identifying where authority should reside.

Higher education provides another example of the influence of context on governance. Colleges and universities narrow the meaning of governance to specific roles of faculty and administrators. Governance committees are formed to deal with prescribed questions and tasks, such as a review of faculty bylaws, or proper representation of faculty on committees. Faculty governance clarifies and limits the topics over which professors have jurisdiction, such as admissions policies and graduation requirements. This definition of governance implies or even prescribes that governing is limited to a task and a formally designated group.

Trying to assign governance to a committee or to limit who is responsible for certain decisions makes sense from the viewpoint of organizational efficiency. However, it initiates competition over ascribed and achieved power while alienating those who are not formally involved. In this tradition, Allison and Dalston define governance in academic settings as distinctly different from management: "Governance is rarely defined but when attempts are made to characterize governance, the definitions are usually vague and not in accord, and most fail to distinguish governance from management."[8] But management and governance are not distinctly different functions. If governance is a system for making public decisions, managers are powerful political actors in that system. Extensive research in public agencies shows that clear distinctions between managing and policy making are unrealistic.[9] Policies and their underlying ideas and values are influenced and shaped by the process of managerial interpretation and implementation. Managers are not neutral agents. They play key roles in decision making and consequently in governance through the latitude of their authority in implementing public programs. The policy shaping role of school principals, who are not formally defined as policy makers, is also well documented in educational settings.[10]

Studies of the importance of context in governance uncover an interesting political paradox for individuals in middle management positions. A school principal must act as a decisive *governor* in certain instances in order to maintain a safe and productive learning environment. However, school principals are not perceived as having governance authority in the context of a school board meeting. Administrators are required to adjust their definition of governing authority to fit the political environment.

## GOVERNANCE AS PUBLIC DISCUSSION

Democratic governance relies on a public dialogue to achieve consensus around common interests. Public deliberation is so fundamental to the process of governing that it has been institutionalized in all modern democracies, with elaborate codes of electoral, parliamentary, administrative, and judicial procedures. Political philosophers have argued that democratic government in essence is a system of governing by discussion:

> *The process of discussion develops sequentially in separate but interconnected forums: in political parties, as they formulate their programs and identify the issues for electoral debate; in the electorate, as it discusses issues and candidates, and expresses a majority in favor of one of the programs; in the legislature, where the majority attempts to translate the programs into law, in constant debate with the opposition; in the executive branch, where the discussion of new policies is carried forward to the chief executive and the cabinet; and in the courts, where the adversary system provides powerful incentives for agencies and interested parties to present the strongest arguments for their respective positions.*[11]

Language is an important yet elusive dimension of governance. Style as well as substance counts, and the words policy makers use as tools to argue for or against programs and proposals help shape their agendas and illuminate their values. The conversation itself *governs* governance, by including and rewarding those who can "talk the talk" and discouraging those who are less articulate or politically literate.

From this perspective, the language of administration and policy limits and controls the way governance works. In formal governance circles, the dialogue is framed within the language of educational administration and policy. William Foster's critical review of educational administration identifies the type of language that can be legitimately used within an administrative context.[12] When administration is defined as a science, the vocabulary is muted and limited to rational and mechanistic arguments. Foster argues that the vocabulary of administrative science perpetuates bureaucratic systems that do not completely fit the nature of schools as social settings. The "school as a factory" metaphor implies that governance should reflect the values of hierarchy, specialization, and control. Schlecty's metaphor of "schools as hospitals" signifies the concern that schools should respond to the pain and suffering of children in urban industrial environments.[13]

Researchers have discovered that the quality and character of a dialogue influences how people construct reality: "knowledge is not a collection of discrete instances of truths; knowledge is, rather, what people create, what they express, in discourses. Discourses create knowledge."[14] Discourse is a system with its own rules that subtly control what can be said within a particular context. Discourse is composed of a group of statements, metaphors, and phrases that belong to a system of knowledge. Administrative and political discourse, for example, are different from discourse in engineering or the arts.

The apparent decline in the quality of public discourse has alienated many citizens from public institutions. Political parties attack and undercut their opponents' positions. Experts from narrowly defined interest groups detail why an organization's programs will not work. Self-appointed citizens committees claim to know how and when tax dollars are being wasted. Like many observers of American politics, the pollster David Yankelovich is concerned about the deterioration of public life and most peoples' lack of involvement in self-governance: "The main precondition to self-governance (and perhaps to global survival) is the simple, fundamental ability to communicate with each other across the barriers of individual differences in interests, nationalities, cultures, and frameworks for the purpose of setting common goals and the strategies for achieving them."[15] Yankelovich believes that the essence of governing is communication about differences between people of good will. He uses the terms *public judgment* and *self-governance* interchangeably. Governance is a system of public judgment and decision making. Effective governance requires civic dialogue, one that builds communities through public trust. Governance occurs in the public dialogue, and language is a real source of power. This definition suggests that effective participants in governance are effective public communicators.

Because schooling involves the exchange of information, ideas, and knowledge, discussions about educational governance are heavily influenced by symbolic language. The public schools play a particularly important role in nationwide governance because they are expected to prepare future citizens to participate in a democratic dialogue.

# GOVERNANCE AS A POLICY PROCESS

Public policies are the outcomes of governance, the codified and legally organized statements and declarations of public authority. Policies are fundamentally public decisions that take shape through procedures, programs, and services.

Studies of the policy process help explain how governance systems work. The policy sciences draw from many disciplines to offer theories, models, and methods to understand and evaluate public policies. Easton's political systems model is a widely accepted approach to simplifying the policy process. Easton describes how inputs, in the form of ideas or concerns with popular support, are converted via a political system (Congress, courts, city councils) into outputs, which are policies and programs.[16] This model defines public policies as fundamentally authoritative decisions. Governance is the public system for making those decisions. Consequently, decision making theories are a big part of the policy sciences, used to explain how and why participants in governance decide between competing interests and values.

Models that describe the policy process can be helpful in their ability to make sense out of the complexity of democratic decision making. Most public decisions are made in complex and idiosyncratic ways. Kindgon's model attempts to capture this complexity, while pointing out three common phases in the policy process:

1. Problem recognition—Specific problems at a local level take on wider public importance, along with advocates and constituent groups as they are acknowledged as state, regional, and even national problems.
2. Policy formulation and refinement—Elected and appointed public officials, along with issue specific experts (e.g., health care experts for health care policies) get involved in shaping the way policies are designed to respond to perceived problems.
3. Politics—Actors in the policy process, including advocacy groups, elected officials, and program administrators, work through the details of program implementation, evaluation, and refinement.[17]

Governance systems take shape within these three phases. Governance structures are the relatively stable patterns of political process that shape the conduct of public affairs in both the public and the private sector. Governance occurs through policy routines and policy systems. Policy routines represent the usual way public decisions are made. One example is the budgeting process in public agencies, in which a uniform and routine pattern of budgeting, accounting, and reporting exists. Policy systems are the more formal structures of governance, such as the separation of powers and the federalist system, which define the powers of both public and private agencies.[18] Examples include the regulation of trade and commerce in the private sector, and the role of the courts in adjudicating Constitutional rights, both in public organizations and in private life.

The policy process reflects many efforts to use rational and logical approaches to solving public problems. Political scientists and systems consultants apply cost/benefit ratios to help determine whether scarce tax dollars should be spent on a public works project or a human services program. At the same time, the policy process in a democratic society is loaded with emotional, political, symbolic, and not all together rational forces. The resulting contradictions in approaches have confused scores of administrators and derailed many well-designed programs.

The variety of approaches to formulating public policy are contained within six general categories or theories of decision making:[19]

- Rationalism—Decisions are derived from logical procedures that objectively consider the costs and benefits of the resulting policy or program. Principles and practices from economics and the policy sciences are applied.
- Incrementalism—Decisions are built on historical precedent, political expediency, and the need to limit changes to marginal differences in existing policies and programs.
- Elite Theory—Public decisions are made by a small number of powerful elites in a given community. Informed experts and powerful private interests are ultimately responsible for making policy choices, in part by shaping mass opinion.
- Institutionalism—Even though policies are initially generated by elected officials or policy boards, they are shaped and fundamentally altered by organizations in the process of implementation. Institutions exist longer than any one policy maker or political administration, and they slowly but surely alter formal policies to shape their institutional values and norms.
- Group Theory—Group interaction is the central fact of politics, and individuals are important as members of interest groups. Decisions are made by managing group conflict and arranging and enforcing compromises.
- Systems Theory—An identifiable set of institutions and activities in society function to transform demands into decisions requiring public support. The system preserves itself by producing reasonably satisfying outputs and through the enforcement of laws and regulations.

These six models of public decision making demonstrate the diversity of ways in which American governance actually takes place. Each approach suggests different sets of participants and procedures designed to influence public decisions, overtly in the case of powerful elites, or covertly in the cultural forces of large systems.

## GOVERNANCE AS A POLITICAL GAME

The language and metaphors of athletic competition and the military are often used to explain the complexities of governance. People speak of playing political games while the popular press depicts winners and losers in the struggles between special interests, politicians, and government bureaucrats. If you decide to attain elected public office, you are *in the race*. Borrowing from the jargon of military history, public agencies are advised to clarify their *mission, tactics,* and *strategies*. Administrators are advised not to "choke" or become disoriented by the political battles at the office.

Organizational consultants simplify the dynamics of power in organizations by developing behavioral theories based on games.[20] Competition, they say, is the creative force behind the American free-market system and games the pastime of popular culture. The educational policy process has been explored through the ecology of games.[21] Teachers make *end runs* around administrators and policy makers in order to teach in a way that they prefer. State and local school board members believe they are *calling the plays*. Problems occur when the players in the schools do not agree on the goals or ground rules designed by people on the sidelines or in the stands.

There are serious problems with this approach to understanding governance. One concern is its fundamentally competitive, win-loose quality. Because governance focuses on public concerns, it requires an element of cooperation and consensus. Thinking of politics and governance only as a game trivializes its broad, public purpose. If it's just a game, politics is not to be taken seriously, adding to the cynicism many Americans already feel about government in general.

## GOVERNANCE AS A SYSTEM

Given the multitude of influences, actors, levels, and relationships within a democratic society, governance needs to be examined within a systems perspective. Systems theories were originally developed as a response to social and organizational complexity and ambiguity. Systems theories provide a more flexible and inclusive view of organizations than the machine-like metaphor. A system by definition is composed of 1) separate and distinguishable components—differentiation—and 2) interaction among these components in order to perform certain functions.[22] The language of systems theory has become a routine part of everyday speech. For example, the term *feedback* is frequently used to describe opinions or critiques. A *feedback loop* in systems theory refers to information used to continually monitor a system's internal operations and its relationship with its environment. Other principles such as entropy and dynamic equilibrium have been incorporated into the lexicon of organizational consultants, academics, and managers to help understand the complexity of social organizations.

Systems theorists point out that no specific component of a system can be described in isolation from another. In public education, for example, a school system cannot be effectively described or understood as separate from teaching and teachers, students, facilities, parents, and most importantly, by observing the interaction of these components. Education reformers have emphasized that a holistic, open systems approach is critical for effective educational reform. "At the very least, we need to treat educational organizations as complex social organisms held together by symbolic webbing rather than as formal systems driven by goals, official roles, commands, and rules."[23] As obvious as this view of public education may sound, there are continuing efforts to reform schools by defining them as simple, machine-like constructs, such as factories or small businesses.

Systems theories have also provided the basis for a shift in school reform from top-down educational policies to questioning the *systems* of educational governance. Chubb and Moe state: "If one really believes that schools are open systems, bad organizational properties must be understood as symptoms rather than causes. The fundamental causes are probably in the environment, and it is there that theory and research on school effectiveness ought to focus."[24] Using a systems approach, they define the *environment* as the decision making system outside of the schools, particularly the school district system, with elected school boards and district-wide administrators.

Thinking about governance from a systems perspective incorporates all the previous definitions of governance into a broad and more detailed approach. A governance system is then composed of both formal structures and the informal aspects of interpersonal communications. It takes into account the politically charged policy process and the context of the organization, activity, or population involved. Defining governance from a systems perspective allows for the level of complexity and scope necessary for a thorough understanding of educational governance.

## CONTEMPORARY DEFINITIONS

Governance can be defined in a way that reflects its complexity as well as the changes in American politics that have occurred in the last few decades. Political scientists and public administrators are now defining governance as an interactive process of governing, which includes more actors than formal government organizations. Governance is an inclusive system that reflects the complexities of multiple actors and constituents competing for public and private resources. Governance is the process by which communities solve problems and meet the needs of their members in a public and participatory setting. Government is the institution generally used for these purposes.[25]

The political economist Louis Weschler's matrix of four sectors of participants is a graphic way to define modern governance.[26] Weschler argues that four distinct groups are involved in governance, from the national to the local level: government agencies, the private sector, nonprofit organizations, and the media. These four categories include the organizations and their representatives. They are all active participants in public decision making, even though one or more of these sectors may not accept or acknowledge their presence and potential power (see Table 2.1).

Weschler's research on the interaction of these four groups demonstrates how decisions are most often made. Government's role is the most obvious and consistent. State and local agencies are the convenors for public decision making and the front line recipients of those decisions. Thus, because of their strong legal and tax supported positions, government agencies are generally considered directly responsible for public policies.

The private sector is involved in public decision making in a variety of ways. Representatives from business and industry are consistently appointed to advisory committees for public agencies and projects. Schools

**TABLE 2.1  Local Level Participants in Governance**

|  | Education | Transportation | Public Safety |
|---|---|---|---|
| Government | School District System | County and City Agencies | County and City Agencies |
| Private Sector | Business Advisory Groups | Contractors Architects Energy Companies | Concerned Businesses Private Security |
| Nonprofits— Special Interest Groups | PTAs Teacher Unions School Foundations Religious Groups | Neighborhood Groups Environmental Organizations | Neighborhood Groups |
| Media | Local and Regional TV Radio Print Material | Local and Regional TV Radio Print Material | Local and Regional TV Radio Print Material |

and universities have established partnerships and cooperative agreements with corporations and small businesses. Public officials from school principals to governors seek the input of the business community when they make policy decisions. Increasingly, public agencies are privatizing and relying on private sector assistance for programs and services that serve the public interest. Small businesses and corporations are also indirectly involved in governance as taxpayers and users of government services.

The nongovernmental, nonprofit sector is a relatively new participant in governance. Nonprofit agencies serve the public interest by providing goods and services. Contract agencies such as United Way and the Red Cross follow governmental rules and regulations and operate with some public funding. But they are separate from government, both through their organizational structures and their representatives. There are multitudes of nonprofit organizations focusing on special interests and representing various segments of society. These groups are more obvious participants in governance debates when they are associated with lobbying and political action. As lobbyists, their representatives are specifically directed to influence the public decision making process, which is another way of saying they are supposed to participate in governance. The nonprofit sector includes large and diverse categories of organizations including research centers, think tanks, colleges and universities, and citizens' advocacy groups.

The number of interest groups involved in governance has been growing for decades. There is an increasing need for different kinds of organizations to get into the public debate, due to the complexity of public problems. Peirces' study of metropolitan governance in large urban centers across the country emphasized that modern problems require more than governmental responses: ". . . it was critical that a region simultaneously develop ways to draw all manner of other players into region-wide problem solving. Major business groups, nonprofits, citizen organizations, universities, and foundations are indispensable participants. Cumulatively, working with government, they become *the* governance structure of the region."[27]

The media is the fourth category or sector involved in governance. Many question the appropriateness of the media as an active player in governance. Yet studies of the growing influence of television and how it presents news stories lends credence to the idea that the media, perhaps unwittingly, is a participant and not a neutral observer.[28] The media affects public policy in a variety of subtle and complex ways. Television, radio, and newspaper coverage of issues has been tracked and correlated with the general public's attention to and interest in various issues. Thus, the length and depth of coverage of an issue helps determine whether public policies will be initiated. Elected officials are highly sensitive to public opinion and shape policies around media-generated polls and surveys.

There are challenges within this collaborative, multi-sector approach to governance and leadership. Portrayed as radical democracy or as a free for all approach to governance, it suggests that no individual or single organization is in charge of anything. If everyone who organizes to exercise public authority and to participate in governance is allowed to do so, authority becomes so dispersed and divided that no one group or organization has enough authority to govern. As Yankelovich observes, "As our society is presently organized, few institutions are responsible for the common interest."[29]

This multi-sector governance environment requires different administrative skills than the command and control approaches used in bureaucratic and hierarchical settings. Public administrators must be able to understand and access networks of decision makers and place greater value on consensus and collaborative decision making. Chapter 4 uses this four-sector model to identify the multiple actors in educational governance. Chapter 7 describes the skills and political competencies needed in a complex governance environment. The remainder of the book draws on a systems perspective and the more inclusive definitions of governance and governing. Citizens in democratic communities need to think about governance in constructive ways and consider themselves as governors in public education.

## SUMMARY

Governance is more than government. It includes both formal structures and informal exchanges between a wide variety of participants. Because of its complexity and scope, American governance is often controversial and defined from several different perspectives:

- Structural—Decisions are made by elected and appointed public officials. Emphasis is on formal relationships between branches and levels of government.
- Contextual—The organization and its activities determine the nature and scope of governance. Governance is delegated to specialized groups or committees.
- Public Discourse—Governance is discussion, debate, and decision making between people with individual differences about common goals.
- Public Policy Process—Governance is the process of recognizing problems, formulating policies, and eventually working through the political issues of program implementation, evaluation, and refinement.
- Political Game—Governance is about competition, winners and losers. The political game requires an insider's understanding of the rules and the goals.

- Systems—Separate and distinguishable components of the governance system interact in order to perform certain functions. No component of the system can be effectively described in isolation from another. Governance systems include all the previous perspectives of governance, plus their interaction.
- Contemporary—Governance is the interactive process of governing, and it includes an increasing variety of interest groups and sectors of society. Collaboration, networking, and consensus are favored over hierarchical control and structure.

Although these seven perspectives contain similar elements, they represent different political values and attitudes about public services. Defining governance from a systems perspective allows for the level of complexity and scope necessary for a thorough understanding of American governance.

## SEMINAR QUESTIONS

1. How do you think most educators define governance? What is the role of classroom teachers in educational governance?

2. Do you believe the media plays an influential role in community governance? How would you improve the media's role in governance?

3. Is there an effective way to balance democratic participation in governance with the need for efficiency in making administrative decisions?

## SUGGESTED READINGS

Cayer, Joseph and Louis F. Weschler. *Public Administration: Social Change and Adaptive Management.* New York: St. Martin's Press, 1988.

Kingdon, John. *Agendas, Alternatives, and Public Policies.* Boston: Little, Brown & Co., 1984.

Osborne, David and Ted Gaebler. *Reinventing Government.* New York: Addison-Wesley, 1992.

Reich, Robert B., ed. *The Power of Public Ideas.* Cambridge, Mass.: Harvard University Press, 1988.

## ENDNOTES

1. Harold D. Laswell, *Politics: Who Gets What, When, How* (New York: Peter Smith, 1950).

2. John C. Calhoun, *A Disquisition on Government* (New York: Peter Smith, 1943).

3. Thomas R. Dye, *American Federalism: Competition Among Governments* (Lexington, Mass.: Lexington Books, 1990).

4. Daniel Yankelovich, *Coming to Public Judgment* (Syracuse, NY: Syracuse University Press, 1991), pp. 101–105. E. J. Dionne, *Why Americans Hate Politics* (Needham Heights, Mass.: Simon & Schuster, 1991).

5. Henry G. Cisneros, "Revitalizing Citizen Activism and Participatory Democracy," *National Civic Review*, vol. 80, no. 1 (Winter 1991) p. 5.

6. David K. Cohen and Deborah L. Ball, "Relations Between Policy and Practice: A Commentary," *Educational Evaluation and Policy Analysis*, vol. 12 no. 3 (Fall, 1990): pp. 249–256. Linda Darling-Hammond, "Instructional Policy into Practice: "The Power of the Bottom Over the Top," *Educational Evaluation and Policy Analysis*, vol. 12, no. 3 (Fall, 1990) pp. 233–241.

7. Hendrik Gideonse, "The Governance of Teacher Education and Systemic Reform," *Educational Policy*, vol. 7 (1993), 402–403.

8. Robert F. Allison and Jeptha W. Dalston, "Governance of University-Owned Teaching Hospitals" (Inquiry 19, Spring 1982), p. 2.

9. Mark Moore, "What Sort of Ideas Become Public Ideas?" *The Power of Public Ideas* (Cambridge: Ballinger Publishing Co., 1988), pp. 55–83. Also see Charles Lindblom, *The Policy-Making Process* (Englewood Cliffs: Prentice-Hall, 1968) and Jeffrey L. Pressman and Aaron Wildavsky, *Implementation* (Berkeley: University of California Press, 1973).

10. David K. Cohen and Deborah L. Ball, "Relations Between Policy and Practice: A Commentary," *Educational Evaluation and Policy Analysis*, vol. 12, no. 3 (Fall 1990), pp. 249–256. Linda Darling-Hammond, "Instructional Policy into Practice: The Power of the Bottom Over the Top," in *Educational Evaluation and Policy Analysis*, vol. 12, no. 3 (Fall 1990), pp. 233–241.

11. Giandomenico Majone, "Policy Analysis and Public Deliberation," in *The Power of Public Ideas*, ed. Robert B. Reich (Cambridge, Mass.: Ballinger Publishing, 1988), p. 159.

12. William Foster, "A Critical Perspective on Administration and Organization in Education," in *Critical Perspectives on the Organization and Improvement of Schooling*, eds. Kenneth A. Sirotnik and Jeannie Oakes (Boston: Kluver-Nijhoff Publishing, 1986), pp. 95–129.

13. Phillip C. Schlechty, *Schools for the Twenty-First Century: Leadership Imperatives for Educational Reform* (San Francisco: Jossey-Bass, 1990).

14. Ginette Delandshere and Anthony R. Petrosky, "Capturing Teachers' Knowledge: Performance Assessment," *Educational Research*, vol. 23, no. 5 (June-July 1994), pp. 11–18.

15. Daniel Yankelovich, *Coming to Public Judgment*, p. 223.

16. David Easton, *A Systems Analysis of Political Life*, (Chicago: University of Chicago Press, 1965), p. 32.

17. John Kingdon, *Agendas, Alternatives, and Public Policies* (Boston: Little, Brown & Co., 1984), pp. 19–21.

18. Barry Bozeman, *All Organizations are Public* (San Francisco: Jossey-Bass, 1989), pp. 66.

19. Thomas R. Dye, *Understanding Public Policy*, 4th ed, (Englewood Cliffs, NJ: Prentice-Hall, 1981). Herbert A. Simon, *Administrative Behavior: A Study of*

*Decision-Making Processes in Administrative Organizations*, 3rd ed. (New York: Free Press, 1976). Charles Lindblom, *The Policy-Making Process* (Englewood Cliffs, NJ: Prentice-Hall, 1968).

20. Jeffrey Pfeffer, *Power in Organizations* (Marshfield: Pitman Publishing, 1981), pp. 1–32. Graham T. Allison, *Essence of Decision* (Boston: Little Brown & Co., 1971), p. 175.
21. William A. Firestone, "Educational Policy as an Ecology of Games," *Educational Researcher*, vol. 18, no. 7 (1989) pp. 18–24.
22. Fremont E. Kast and James E. Rosenzweig, "General Systems Theory: Applications for Organization and Management," *Academy of Management Journal* (December 1972), pp. 447–465.
23. Terrence Deal, "Reframing Reform," *Educational Leadership* (May 1990), p. 7.
24. John E. Chubb and Terry M. Moe, *Politics, Markets, and America's Schools* (Washington, DC: Brookings, 1991), p. 19.
25. David Osborne and Ted Gaebler, *Reinventing Government* (New York: Addison-Wesley, 1992).
26. N. Joseph Cayer and Louis F. Weschler, *Public Administration: Social Change and Adaptive Management.* (New York: St. Martin's Press, 1988). Also see Paul C. Bauman and Louis F. Weschler, "The Rocky Mountain Program: Advanced Learning for the Complexities of Public Management," *Public Productivity & Management Review*, vol. XV, no. 4 (1992), pp. 463–475. Weschler has assisted in the design of several executive development programs for public managers, incorporating the four-sector approach to forming leadership groups and designing curricula.
27. Neal R. Peirce, *Citistates* (Washington, DC: Seven Locks Press, 1993), p. 317.
28. John Kingdon, *Agendas, Alternatives, and Public Policies* (Boston: Little, Brown & Co., 1984), pp. 61–64. Christopher Lasch, "Journalism, Publicity, and the Lost Art of Argument," *Gannett Center Journal* (Spring 1990), pp. 1–11.
29. Daniel Yankelovich, *Coming to Public Judgment*, p. 241.

# 3

# A BRIEF HISTORY
# OF SCHOOL GOVERNANCE

*New histories usually appear either because
the discovery of new sources demands the
rewriting of old accounts or because new
purposes demand the reorganization of familiar materials to meet new requirements.*
—John Brubacher, Educational Historian, 1947.

Educational decision making is shaped in part by political traditions, social values, and organizational agreements that developed over the decades of American history. This chapter briefly summarizes the foundations of educational governance based on a review of six periods in the history of American education.

The value-laden and complex nature of public education requires a review of multiple interpretations of educations past, including sometimes contradictory views of what actually occurred. As the historian Charles Beard noted over fifty years ago: "It is that any selection and arrangement of facts pertaining to any large area of history, either local or world, race or class, is controlled inexorably by the frame of reference in the mind of the selector and arranger."[1] Since Beard's warning in 1934, many new interpretations of the evolution of American education have been written, providing a more informed view of events and issues. By including diverse perspectives, the richness and detail of the schools as social, political, and economic factors in American culture can be better understood. At the same time, these revisions of history generate less certainty about the accuracy of any one interpretation of how the American educational system came to be.

Historians have categorized the foundations of American education into eras, epochs, critical events, structural changes, political cycles, and reform movements. Table 3.1 presents six formative periods in the history of American education. These time frames are reflections of general trends that are particularly relevant to school and system-wide governance. They are presented as summaries of educational movements, not as distinct periods in time or separations of predominant ideologies. Readers are encouraged to refer to the texts and historical accounts listed as suggested readings at the end of this chapter for greater detail and definition of the events and actors who shaped American education.

## IMPLICATIONS OF SIX HISTORICAL PERIODS

Each period in the history of American education added organizational structures and social values to the next generation of schools. However, viewing historical developments as a cumulative process can be deceptive, suggesting a constructive progression of ideas and institutions. There are many underlying tensions, inconsistencies, and contradictions that must also be considered in a system as large as American education. Given the public nature of America's schools, there has always been an element of political debate and compromise. As Kastle states: "what appears to be an American consensus on education is to some extent the result of ambivalence, muted conflict, and trade-offs. The American public schools are a gigantic, standardized compromise most of us have learned to live with."[2] Within the domain of compromise and conflict, certain themes and trends can be identified that help explain the present context of educational governance.

**Public Education Has a Strong Tradition of Democratic Governance.** As soon as the first American communities formed around economic interests, decisions about schools were made in town meetings or through representative democracies. There were many disenfranchised groups and often autocratic sources of authority; but the schools were important components of the original communities, and democratic decision making has always been a practical concern. Progressive reformers in later generations introduced special governments for schools in the form of school districts and state departments of education, which were again built on the principles of democratic participation in decision making. More recent movements to privatize public education have challenged the utility of democratically elected school boards and public control of schools.

**TABLE 3.1  Formative Periods in the History of American Education**

| Historical Period | Focus of Government | Structural Emphasis | Reform Values | Social, Economic Factors |
|---|---|---|---|---|
| Colonial America: 1600–Revolution | Family Church | Theocratic State Charters Town Council | Private Choice Religious Schools | Rural Populace Agrarian Economy |
| Nation Building: 1789–1870s | Common School | Town Council State Role | National Identity Americanization | Civil Unrest Rural Populace Agrarian Economy |
| Industrial America: 1870–1950s | School Boards Cities | District System Administration State Agencies | Efficiency Order | Industrialization Urbanization Immigration |
| Conflict: 1960s–1970s | Civil Rights Parents and Students | Activist Groups Finance Reform Legal Questions | Equity Participation | Social Unrest Conflict Suburbanization |
| State Reforms: 1983–1992 | States National Interest | State Policies Private Sector Involvement | Excellence Accountability | Cynicism toward Government Information-based Economy |
| Governance Reforms: 1988–Present | Schools Family | Site-based Management Schools of Choice | Excellence Privatization | Globalization Diversity |

However, a vast majority of schools in the United States are still *public* and operate under the principles of democratic participation.

**Educational Governance Has Become Increasingly Complex.** The American system of education has come a long way since the days of the small community school in the eighteenth century. Decades of growth and change have created institutional components that make school structures more rather than less complex, despite district consolidation, decentralization, or centralization.[3] In order to accommodate the demands of external organizations, new departments, new layers of government, or entire agencies have been added to state and local school systems. Educational administration as a widely accepted profession emerged within the twentieth century, bringing technical expertise as well as a new layer of decision making. Public agencies involved in educational governance have been joined by private companies that influence the schools in unregulated and indirect ways, including textbook publishers and testing companies. Special interest groups concerned about issues ranging from taxation to religious freedom are also present in many school governance settings as political forces separate from elected school boards.

The topics of concern within the environment of schools are more complex than many of the issues past generations had to face. Since the late 1940s, school boards and administrators have struggled over attempts at racial balance, sex education, bilingual education, inequitable state funding formulas, voter initiated tax limitations, state and federal mandates, prayer and creationism in schools, and affirmative action requirements.[4] Because public organizations are democratically governed, they are open to the diversity of organizational and individual interests in a modern society. All of these factors contribute to the complexity of educational governance.

**Educational Governance Has Always Been Political and Controversial.** As noted in Chapter 1, governance involves politics, power, and decision-making authority. Educators and policy makers have disagreed for decades about the best way to balance political authority. One of the vestiges of education's 200-year history is the ongoing tension between two views of authority and control. The original colonists built schools under the auspices of a theocratic or central state authority, which evolved into a secular state in the form of state governments and large district systems. The investment in state-level reform in the 1980s and national goals and standards in the 1990s are strong testimonies to the continued belief in centralized political authority. The opposing view maximizes democratic participation and decentralized control. In a somewhat contradictory fashion, the United States has chosen to pursue both approaches simultaneously. In a federalist system political power is decentralized and distributed to states and local school districts, while the authority of the state and federal levels of government continue to operate as centralizing forces. Reforms aimed at school-based decision making in the 1980s and 1990s have inevitably renewed the tensions between centralized and decentralized governance.

Another way of deciphering the political quality of education's history is the persistence of ideology in school reform. Efforts to improve education have generally included broad social and political agendas. Consider the political ramifications of the nineteenth century movement to build common schools and a common curriculum in order to unify an entire continent of people. The federal government promoted science and mathematics education in order to compete with the Soviet Union in the race for space. As Tyack observed: "The history of American public schools is rich in visions of possibility, beginning with the evangelists of Horace Mann's generation. Leaders such as John Dewey and Martin Luther King Jr. expressed a powerful commitment to social justice that energized their contemporaries."[5] The agenda for the public schools in the 1990s reflects a continuing belief that education can accomplish broad social, political, and economic goals.

**Educational Governance May Be Outdated.**    Changes in demographics, advances in technology, and diversification in the economy suggest it may be time to update the structures and traditions of educational decision making. Many of the components of state and local governance have remained essentially the same since their creation in the last century. Procedures and policies governing district-state relations and district-school relations have not been modified to support new approaches to site-based decision making and participatory management. As Deal points out: "Historical educational practices are not always equal to the demands of a modern society. . . . Technology, demographic shifts, new economic challenges, and other forces call to question many traditional educative forms and practices."[6]

These implications are derived from a review of the six periods in the history of American education. The legal, political, and organizational outcomes of each successive period are more complex than the previous era, coinciding with the growth and development of American institutions and ideas. The most recent periods in the history of educational governance are described in the context of governance reform in Chapter 6.

# FORMATIVE PERIODS IN THE HISTORY OF AMERICAN EDUCATION

## Colonial America: 1600–1776

Many of the original colonists came to the American continent in pursuit of religious and political freedoms after generations of persecution and struggle in Europe. Entire communities in New England were formed on the basis of common religious beliefs and customs. The colonies were not yet autonomous political agents but rather clusters of small towns and farms in different geographical regions. Schools were established and governed by agreements set forth in educational charters, granted to families in a given locale by religious leaders and colonial proprietors. The control of schools, curricula, and teachers rested in the hands of the churches and clergy who predominated in a particular region.[7] Education was essentially a family concern and schools were predominantly religious, private, and selective.

Even though schools were small and operated by local groups, governance authority was still granted by a theocratic *state*, a political entity represented by the power of a king, or colonial legislature. There was no clear distinction between church and state. Colonial legal codes were based on British law and customs in which the state retained political authority over most aspects of education. The sovereignty of the *state* in colonial America, and more specifically the Massachusetts Education Laws of 1642 and 1647, created the legal basis for a state system of schools that followed in the nineteenth century.[8]

The demand for an education that provided more than religious training intensified when small towns began to form around economic activities. Schools were needed to teach trades and practical skills that served the community. Governance traditions that developed vested the control of education in lay boards which could be more responsive to community interests than distant religious or political authorities. Boards of governors were established to regulate curricula, hire or fire teachers, and levy taxes from both the community and parents. This first system of school governance worked well in areas that were homogeneous, but as different religious groups began to converge in larger towns and cities, community-based control became problematic. Private schools expanded as many parents demonstrated their desire to instill their own values for their children aside from the economic and occupational concerns of community schools.

## Nation-Building: 1776–1865

The American Revolution and formation of a federalist system of government marks the beginning of the second era in American education.

The period between the American Revolution and the Civil War (1776 to 1865) has been depicted as a time of nation-building.[9] When the colonies became an autonomous nation, they were deeply committed to preserving the democracy they had won in battle and codified in law. Elected leaders wanted to create a process by which an isolated, rural populace could be prepared to accept and carry out the duties of citizenship. At the same time, the founding fathers would not permit a national government to use the schools as vehicles for propaganda.[10] Consequently, the U.S. Constitution did not establish a national educational system or mention schools in any way. The newly created federalist system empowered state governments to establish schools and other kinds of public services. Legally, states were granted the authority but not a clear direction or any form of financial support for schools. The federal role in education has expanded over the last two hundred years through other Constitutional provisions, particularly Article I, Section 8, which gives Congress the power to "provide for the common defense and general welfare." However, the federal government's role in American schools is still limited and controversial.

The development of public education between the American Revolution and the Civil War was heavily influenced by the threat of civil unrest and the need to establish a stable nation and an effective civil government. Common schooling was promoted by reformers in order to establish a common ideology and a common culture to unite the diverse interests of immigrants and isolated communities of settlers. Jefferson's efforts in the Virginia legislature were based on the principle that education is critical to the survival of a democracy and should therefore be in the control of state and local governments, as opposed to the federal government or private, religious, and sectarian agencies. Jefferson and other prominent educators, including Henry Barnard and Horace Mann, argued that schools should be supported with public funds raised through local taxes. Mann in particular argued that the state should be a higher authority in its relationship with smaller jurisdictions, with the ability to set minimum curricular and financial standards for local districts.[11] Mann envisioned a partnership between local schools and state governments who were essential forces in directing the content of a common educational experience. Toward this end, the first state-level boards of education were established by Mann in Massachusetts and Barnard in Connecticut.

Local control remained strong particularly in the south where county government autonomy was respected while centralized governments were unpopular. Many people believed that state bureaucracy and regulations were unnecessary when schools were inexpensively created and governed in rural America. The Protestant Reformation questioned the propriety of paying taxes for other peoples' children, believing education was a religious right and a family matter. There is disagreement among historians over the degree to which the general public in the nineteenth century was supportive of the movement to create common schools and state roles in public education. The views of the so-called consensus historians, which prevailed until the 1950s, reflected a belief that most Americans were supportive of free public education, portraying a benevolent and egalitarian American tradition of public schools.[12] More recently, revisionist historians have argued that from a political perspective, early reformers were dangerously engaged in social control, convinced that their goal of *Americanization* could not be achieved without some persuasive forces over the populace, particularly the new immigrants and the poor.[13]

The United States was predominantly an agrarian society in the 1800s and most schools were still private and religious. Small community-based school districts began to appear, based on old colonial provisions that permitted school districts to be formed almost anywhere a few families wished to establish a school and levy taxes. In this period, schools were under the direction of the town council and school management was performed by lay citizens.[14] Educational governance was controlled by small general governments. Schlecty characterized a school in this period as the "tribal center designed to induct the young into the traditions of the tribe. Citizenship and cultural enlightenment became the basis for the school curriculum. The curriculum became, in effect, a repository of the lore of the republic—the white, Anglo-Saxon, Protestant republic, and the school became the center of the tribe or, more accurately, the center of the community that was assumed to exist and which it was assumed the schools were designed to serve."[15]

Although legal authority for school districts and boards was originally established by the Massachusetts Education Laws in 1642 and 1647, special governments for education took shape across the country in the 1800s, assuming the education-related responsibilities of town councils. Beginning in New York in 1812, state level departments began to take shape, often including a chief state school officer, known at the time as the state superintendent of public instruction. State boards of education were appointed to oversee the preparation of teachers and to provide technical services for local schools. Legal rulings and legislative ordinances codified and strengthened state and local educational structures. Massachusetts was the first state to officially adopt publicly funded education in 1826, followed by Vermont in 1854 and Connecticut in 1856.[16] The separation between church and state was advanced in large part by a ruling in a New York court in 1842 which declared that no school in which any religious sectarian doctrine or tenet was taught would be eligible for public funds. By the 1860s, many of the structural components of state departments of education and local school districts had been organized.

## Industrial America: 1865–1950s

America's only civil war profoundly changed public perception of government and private enterprise. The Civil War was waged between two different cultural and economic systems: an urban, industrial society in the North opposing a decentralized, agrarian economy in the slave holding South. The Northern victory established the sovereignty of a federalist system of government and demonstrated the resilience of an industrialized and more centralized economy. The Industrial Revolution, the development of capitalism, and urbanization quickly followed. The Western frontier was aggressively settled while state and local governments were being organized on the political and legal principles of the original northern states. The turn of the century is widely recognized as a period of rapid and unprecedented population growth, driven by a large influx of immigrants. The population grew from just over 30 million in 1860 to over 100 million by 1920.[17] Heterogeneous groups of non-English speaking immigrants and unprecedented demands in the new industrial economy suddenly challenged the capacity and structure of an educational system that was still in its formative stages.

The combined effects of industrialization and population growth initiated the reorganization, redefinition, and unprecedented expansion of American education. The dimensions of growth in schooling during this period are symbolic of what has been called the "American Century." In 1890 only seven percent of the eligible age group went to high school and only one percent to college. Within an eighty year period, ninety percent of Americans aged fourteen to seventeen were in high school.[18] Causal factors include compulsory attendance laws, state funding, rapidly changing occupational environments, the advent of the school bus, and new social norms supporting education. This expansion was facilitated by the creation of large, urban school districts as well as the continued growth of small districts in towns and cities in the new Western states.

The effects of the industrial revolution went far beyond the creation of factories and assembly-line production methods. Labor markets, distribution systems, and the modern conception of bureaucratic organizations emerged. Industrialization attempted to establish a clear sense of order, rationality, and scientific efficiency for organizational structures, for decision making, and for work habits.[19] Top-down decision making and accountability structures were established, along with social divisions between the managers and the managed.[20] These developments in the economic sector created new challenges for an expanding educational system. The nineteenth century vision of public education as a disseminator of a common culture through common schooling became secondary to the need to respond to developments in industry, science, and their associated occupations.

A combination of economic, scientific, and organizational advances helped shape the progressive movement in public education. The practice of public administration and ideas about democratic politics also changed as a result of the widespread belief in "scientific management." Business leaders wanted to centralize the control of schools, emulating the new models of large corporations. As Sirotnik points out: "It did not take long for this view to be swallowed hook, line, and sinker by educators and educational reformers."[21] The *school as a factory* metaphor was accepted by many administrators: "School leaders, like the industrial leaders they looked to as models and guides, sought the Holy Grail of scientific management. Efficiency became the prime value; differentiation, standardization, control, and rationality became the operating guides."[22] School buildings and administrative hierarchies were modeled after thriving corporations and businesses. As Chapter 6 points out, corporate models and metaphors are still used as points of criticism and prescriptions for school reforms in the 1990s.

This period in history included the development and refinement of state-level educational systems. Progressive reformers promoted a governance design in which state boards of education and chief state school officers would monitor and guide local districts by establishing centralized standards and regulations for teachers, administrators, and facilities. If conflicts between state and local authorities arose, the state view was to prevail. However, the emergence of a strong state role and associated political relationships developed unevenly in different regions of the country. Southern states in particular defended the powers of county and city governments and consistently advocated for local control of schools. Even though state governments and agencies were gaining authority, they were still small in relation to the thousands of local school districts.

By the 1960s, a majority of states had organized similar structures for assisting and overseeing local school districts. State departments of education grew in size and influence and led in the consolidation of rural schools and the enforcement of uniform educational standards. States certified teachers and administrators in an effort to promote efficiency and productivity and to ensure competency. School administrators were required to complete courses on finance, facility maintenance, and personnel management.[23]

Political controversy and change was particularly acute in urban areas. City school systems and city governments quickly became large, differentiated bureaucracies. Lay boards relinquished day-to-day operating responsibilities to professionally trained school administrators. As Tyack noted:

*As decision-making power shifted to superintendents and their staff, the number of specialists and administrators ballooned. School systems*

*grew in size, added tiers of officials, and became segmented into func-*
*tional divisions: elementary, junior high, and high schools; vocational*
*programs of several kinds; classes for the handicapped; counseling ser-*
*vices; research and testing bureaus; and many other departments.*[24]

Along with the growth of urban school districts, state departments of
education, the courts, and the federal government assumed more important roles in setting policies and imposing regulations. The bureaucratization of schooling increased into the 1960s, based on arguments for
efficiency, modern management techniques, specialization of teachers,
broadened curricular offerings, and the larger societal belief in modern-
ized public bureaucracies. Relations between state agencies and local districts in this period could be described as partnership oriented, in which
the states were organized to play a limited technical role while leaving
the bulk of decision making authority to local jurisdictions.

Along with a new specialized and departmentalized structure for
schools came the need to redesign outdated governance systems. Until the
1950s, schools were controlled by thousands of small, independent districts. Progressive reformers believed that if authority rested in the hands of
experts instead of local, lay school boards, a more effective kind of accountability could be organized. State and local administrative regulations and
bureaucratic procedures were designed to equalize education through standardization. The progressive approach to governance included the ideals of
corporate management as applied to public institutions, in which smaller,
more orderly school boards would decide policy questions and delegate
administration to specialists, replacing or preventing the corruption, chaos,
and graft assumed to be present in lay politics. Boards in larger cities were
increasingly composed of businessmen and professionals. School districts
still enjoy considerable managerial and fiscal autonomy grounded on the
progressive's belief in the separation of politics and administration, larger
districts, and nonpartisan lay boards of education. This approach predominated as the total number of school districts in the United States shrank
from 127,000 in 1930 to approximately 14,700 in 1989.[25]

School reform in the industrial age was not limited to changes in
governance. The progressives believed that the public schools should
redesign the curricula to respond to the conditions brought about by the
obvious advances in science and industry. They challenged the limiting
and authoritarian qualities of common schools and a common academic
curriculum. The progressives believed that a uniform curriculum was
poorly adapted to the diversity of students from immigrant families. As
Cuban observed: "(progressives) were anxious to fit the curriculum to
the student rather than the student to the curriculum."[26] New courses
and vocational programs were added as schools enlarged and became

more bureaucratic. Emulating the corporate world, curriculum designers approached school systems as if they were engineers who could reduce the full range of human experiences into measurable terms and learning experiences.[27]

There was a dissenting minority of social reformers and scholars throughout the first half of the twentieth century who questioned the bureaucratic and mechanistic approach to managing organizations. It was not until the 1950s that a growing number of social scientists were able to effectively show the down side to the prevailing belief in scientifically managed bureaucracies. Organizational psychologists documented the more complex behavioral aspects of group work. Public administrators began to recognize the politically uncertain and non-quantifiable nature of public agencies and the problems of trying to quantify public services.

In public education, revisionist historians wrote about the problems within bureaucratized schools. They urged reformers and policy makers to move away from an idealized view of the past, pointing to the neglect of pluralism in the schools, unequal educational opportunities, and the conservative nature of bureaucracies. Cohen used blunt political rhetoric in 1957 when he stated: "Most historians of education are now ready to examine the public schools as instruments of social control, giving due regard to their possibly restrictive and coercive functions, and they are willing to disclose phenomena long hidden by official pieties, for example, the maltreatment of immigrants and ethnic groups, the discriminatory treatment of women and minority groups, the connection between schools and politics and between education and social stratification."[28] Studies of these issues followed, as well as politically charged debates about compulsory attendance laws and the socio-economic implications of progressive reforms and scientized schools.

After World War II the courts became influential agencies in educational policy making.[29] Student rights, district personnel policies, and the separation of public and private education were affirmed and clarified through a series of judicial decisions. When the U.S. Supreme Court's 1954 ruling known as *Brown vs. the Board of Education* determined that the long accepted *separate but equal* doctrine was in fact not equal and in violation of the Fourteenth Amendment of the Constitution, educational reform moved to the courts. School desegregation, forced busing, and a myriad of social issues and legal battles changed the way educators and policy makers thought about schools and other public institutions. The one-hundred-year period of educational expansion, bureaucratization, and centralization was no longer viewed in the same light.

As public schooling in America expanded in the post war baby boom era, private organizations engaged in printing textbooks and building suburban schools entered the decision making process of school districts. All three branches of state government demonstrated their authority and influence in educational policy making. Public education had grown to become a significant component of the national economy and the largest civic enterprise.

## Conflict: The 1960s and 1970s

The 1960s marked a turning point in education from steady expansion to conflict and uncertainty. Dissatisfaction with schools came from many sources. Critics argued that the curriculum in most schools had become ineffective in providing the nation with scientists and engineers. Katz summarized the most troubling concerns: "Academic critics worried about basic skills; urban reformers complained about blackboard jungles and dull, repressive classrooms; social scientists documented the schools' inability to promote equality; and civil rights activists found the schools not only segregated but racist."[30] After the *Brown vs. Board* decision in 1954, many groups entered school politics at the local level, as federal judges implemented school desegregation orders.

The crisis of confidence in the schools paralleled the criticisms of many political and social movements in the 1960s. Demonstrations against the war in Vietnam undermined many people's belief in the credibility of public institutions and government bureaucracies. Civil rights activists questioned the sincerity of school boards in large cities, where policy makers were seen as distant from the lives of minorities and the poor. Parents demanded that schools become more receptive to alternative teaching methods and changes in the curriculum. Social activists often had different reform agendas but shared the concern that local school boards and district bureaucracies were unresponsive under corporate models designed to take schools out of politics.[31] School administrators faced several unanticipated contradictions. They had been trained to keep politics and partisanship out of education and to be unresponsive to pressure groups. Yet, they were publicly attacked for their isolation and apparent indifference to widely acknowledged social and ethnic inequities. Educational policy makers were caught between the tradition of bureaucratic efficiency and the growing importance of community participation and political activism.[32]

These fundamental challenges to the managerial approaches and professional values of educational administrators disrupted the traditional power structures of school governance without producing a coherent or widely accepted set of alternatives. In many cases, the response of school districts and state and federal agencies to dissent was to bureaucratize critical groups, assigning their representatives to accountability committees and citizens' advisory groups. Tyack's analysis of governance problems in this period reveals some of the causes of conflict that exists today: "The result of the new politics of education in the 1960s was a blending of different forms of governance . . . everybody and nobody was in charge of public schooling in that tumultuous decade. School district leaders lost their sense of control over schooling, but the influence of outsiders was patchy and incomplete."[33] Formal state and local governance structures did not change appreciably during this period. The make-up and selection of governing boards remained essentially the same as in the 1940s. However, the informal dimensions of governance were significantly affected by conflict and tensions between different factions and levels of policy making. Disagreements between administrators and school board members escalated. State departments of education and school district offices were increasingly engaged in disputes over the causes of problems identified by reformers.

Within the framework of school organization and instructional innovation, free schools, open classrooms, flexible scheduling, and middle schools were introduced in this period. By the late 1970s, however, many of these approaches were abandoned when policy makers responded to renewed calls for traditional academic programs, longer school days, more homework, and conventional approaches to teaching.[34]

Criticisms surrounding public institutions and large organizations in the private sector continued in the 1970s. Changes in educational governance were brought about in large part by legal challenges and political conflicts over state and local school finance formulas. Just as taxation of any kind is controversial, public financial support for schools has been an issue throughout the history of American education. In the 1970s, a series of legal rulings in both state and federal courts questioned the equity of school funding arrangements. State legislatures were forced to respond to inequalities between districts, racial and ethnic groups, and special populations. Litigation often strengthened the role of state courts, legislatures, and departments of education in setting educational policies while shifting governance authority away from local school boards.[35]

## State Reforms: The 1980s

A flurry of national reports, task force recommendations, and political summit conferences followed publication of *A Nation at Risk*, which symbolized the serious nature of school reform in the 1980s after the tumultuous and litigious decades of the 1960s and 1970s. An unprecedented number of system-wide reforms were promoted by public, private, and nonprofit organizations. Chapter 6 describes many of the proposed changes in this period, including the impacts of the first and second waves of school reform.

This era of top-down, policy-driven reforms created a new context for governance with the states clearly in the leadership roll.[36] State legislatures passed laws and state departments of education prescribed more courses, more time in classes, and greater accountability in order to improve the American educational system to meet world-class standards. Historians depict a philosophical shift in emphasis from the pursuit of equity to an overriding concern for educational excellence in the 1980s, along with a reconfiguration of interest groups and political authority.[37] Before the end of the 1980s, the centralizing quality of state-generated reforms and top-down policy implementation appeared to be ineffective. Organizational questions about the most effective focus of governance continued.

### Questioning Governance: The 1990s

In the 1990s, more profound changes in governance are being proposed and implemented. After ten years of intense state-level school improvement efforts directed at teaching, learning, and student performance, policy makers are increasingly looking at changing governance structures and procedures. Schools of choice, privatization of public education, and charter schools are contemporary versions of political and structural reforms that were proposed in the past. Tyack observed in 1992: "Once again people are seeking to perfect the schools through changes in governance."[38] The schools continue to be viewed as a vehicle for broad social and economic changes in society, while educators and parents continue to debate the best place and best way to make decisions about education.

The focus of governance reform in the 1990s appears to be centering on the local school district system. A popular movement to school-based decision making, coupled with national goals and standards has placed local districts in an unstable middle ground. Chapters 6, 7, and 8 provide an indication of probable governance reform in the coming years as a result of simultaneous pressures of decentralization and centralization and the cumulative effects of decades of change.

### SUMMARY

Educational governance is the product of six formative periods in the history of American education. The governance systems that developed in the colonial period moved the control of education from private religious interests to town councils and lay boards which could be more responsive to community concerns. The U.S. Constitution did not establish a national educational system or mention schools in any way.

In the 1800s, the newly created federalist system empowered the states to establish schools through the Tenth Amendment. However, the federal government did not provide financial support or a sense of direction or mission for local schools. Common schooling was promoted by reformers in order to establish a common ideology and a common culture to unite the diverse interests of immigrants and isolated communities of settlers. Special governments for education emerged in the form of school boards and districts who assumed the education-related responsibilities of town councils and city governments. The sudden arrival of large numbers of non-English speaking immigrants challenged the capacity and structure of an educational system that was still in its formative stages.

After the Civil War, the combined effects of industrialization and population growth precipitated the reorganization, redefinition, and unprecedented expansion of American education. The nineteenth century vision of public education as a disseminator of a common culture through common schooling was overshadowed by the need to respond to developments in industry, science, and their associated occupations. As the twentieth century began, progressive reformers pushed for the consolidation of small, politically controlled school districts. The progressives promoted a governance design in which state boards of education and chief state school officers would monitor and guide local districts by establishing centralized standards and regulations for teachers, administrators, and facilities.

When the U.S. Supreme Court's 1954 ruling known as *Brown vs. the Board of Education* determined that the long accepted *separate but equal* doctrine was in violation of the Fourteenth Amendment, educational reform moved to the courts. The 1960s marked a turning point in education from steady expansion to conflict and uncertainty. Dissatisfaction with schools came from many sources and the corporate model of educational governance was viewed as insensitive to the concerns of parents and communities. In the 1970s, changes in educational governance were brought about by legal challenges and political conflicts over state and local school finance formulas. The 1980s is widely recognized as a decade of top down, policy-driven reforms, creating a new context for governance with the states clearly in the leadership role. Historians noted a philosophical shift in emphasis from equity to excellence and a reconfiguration of interest groups and political authority. In the 1990s, fundamental governance structures are being challenged, including the utility of democratically elected school boards and the design of the local district system of public schools.

# SEMINAR QUESTIONS

1. Historians offer at least two divergent interpretations of the history of American education:

    (1) The traditionalists' view of democratic support and general consensus about the value and importance of free, public education.

    (2) The revisionists' view that much of what occurred was the result of political conflict, compromise, social control, and considerable injustice along the way.

    What is your view?

2. In your estimation, what are the most important governance trends in the 200-year history of American education?

3. Do you think the present system of locally elected school boards and school districts is democratic and representative of community interests?

# SUGGESTED READINGS

Bellah, Robert N., et al., *The Good Society.* New York: Alfred A. Knopf, 1991.

Porter, Steven. *Wisdoms Passing.* New York: Barclay House, 1989.

Schlechty, Phillip C., *Schools for the Twenty-First Century: Leadership Imperatives for Educational Reform.* San Francisco: Jossey-Bass, 1990.

Tyack, David. "School Governance in the United States: Historical Puzzles and Anomalies." In *Decentralization and School Improvement*, eds. Jane Hannaway and Martin Carnoy. San Francisco: Jossey-Bass, 1993.

Warren, Donald R., ed. *History, Education, and Public Policy.* Berkeley, Calif.: McCutchan Publishing Corporation, 1978.

# ENDNOTES

1. Charles A. Beard, "Written History as an Act of Faith," *American Historical Review*, vol. 39 (1934), p. 227.

2. Carl F. Kaestle, "Conflict and Consensus Revisited: Notes Toward a Reinterpretation of American Educational History," in *History, Education, and Public Policy*, ed. Donald R. Warren (Berkeley, Calif.: McCutchan Publishing Corporation, 1978), p. 314.

3. David K. Cohen, "Governance and Instruction: The Promise of Decentralization and Choice," in *Choice and Control in American Education*, William H. Clune and John F. Witte eds. (New York: Falmer Press, 1990).

4. Steven Porter, *Wisdoms Passing* (New York: Barclay House, 1989), p. 38.

5. David Tyack, "School Governance in the United States: Historical Puzzles and Anomalies," in *Decentralization and School Improvement*, ed. Jane Hannaway and Martin Carnoy (San Francisco: Jossey-Bass, 1993), p. 25.

6. Terrence Deal, "Reframing Reform," *Educational Leadership* (May 1990), p. 9.
7. Porter, *Wisdoms Passing*, p. 30.
8. R. Freeman Butts and Lawrence A. Cremin, *A History of Education in American Culture* (New York: Holt and Company, 1959), p. 13.
9. John S. Brubacher, *A History of the Problems of Education* (New York: McGraw-Hill, 1947). Also see Butts and Cremin, *A History of Education in American Culture.*
10. Jean McGrew, "Developing a Shared Vision: Business, Government and Education," *National Civic Review*, vol. 80, no. 1. (1991), p. 32.
11. Porter, *Wisdoms Passing*, p. 31.
12. Kaestle, "Conflict and Consensus Revisited: Notes Toward a Reinterpretation of American Educational History," in *History, Education, and Public Policy*, p. 309.
13. Maxine Greene, "Identities and Contours: An Approach to Educational History," in *History, Education, and Public Policy*, ed. Donald R. Warren (Berkeley, CA: McCutchan Publishing Corporation, 1978), pp. 296–308.
14. Ronald F. Campbell, et al., *The Organization and Control of American Schools* (Columbus, Ohio: Charles E. Merrill Publishing Co., 1980), p. 9.
15. Phillip C. Schlechty, *Schools for the Twenty-First Century: Leadership Imperatives for Educational Reform* (San Francisco: Jossey-Bass, 1990), p. 18.
16. Porter, *Wisdoms Passing*, p. 31.
17. R. Freeman Butts and Lawrence A. Cremin, *A History of Education in American Culture* (New York: Holt and Company, 1959), p. 293.
18. Robert N. Bellah, et al., *The Good Society* (New York: Alfred A. Knopf, 1991), p. 146.
19. Kenneth A. Sirotnik, "The School as the Center of Change," in *Schooling for Tomorrow: Directing Reforms to Issues That Count*, ed. Thomas J. Sergiovanni and John H. Moore (Boston: Allyn and Bacon, 1989).
20. Michael B. Katz, *Reconstructing American Education.* (Cambridge, Mass.: Harvard University Press, 1987), p. 119.
21. Sirotnik, "The School as the Center of Change," p. 101.
22. Schlechty, *Schools for the Twenty-First Century: Leadership Imperatives for Educational Reform*, pp. 21–22. Schlecty cites R. W. Callahan, *Education and the Cult of Efficiency.* (Chicago: University of Chicago Press, 1963).
23. Larry Cuban, "The District Superintendent and the Restructuring of Schools: A Realistic Appraisal;" in *Schooling for Tomorrow: Directing Reforms to Issues That Count*, ed. Thomas J. Sergiovanni and John H. Moore (Boston: Allyn & Bacon, 1989), p. 262.
24. David B. Tyack, "Ways of Seeing: An Essay on the History of Compulsory Schooling," in *History, Education, and Public Policy*, ed. Donald R. Warren (Berkeley, Calif.: McCutchan Publishing Corporation, 1978), p. 74.
25. Austin D. Swanson and Richard A. King, *School Finance: Its Economics and Politics* (New York: Longman, 1991), p. 42.
26. Larry Cuban, "Reforming Again, Again, and Again," *Educational Researcher* (Washington, DC: American Educational Research Association, January 1990), p. 4.

27. Marie E. Wirsing, "Educational Competence and Wire Cages," *The Educational Forum* (Fall 1982), pp. 9–23.
28. Sol Cohen, "History of Education as a Field of Study: An Essay on Recent Historiography of American Education," in *History, Education, and Public Policy*, ed. Donald R. Warren (Berkeley, Calif.: McCutchan Publishing Corporation, 1978), p. 48.
29. Lawrence Cremin, "More than Schooling," in *History, Education, and Public Policy*, ed. Donald R. Warren (Berkeley, Calif.: McCutchan Publishing Corporation, 1978), pp. 22–53.
30. Katz, *Reconstructing American Education*, p. 111.
31. Tyack, "School Governance in the United States: Historical Puzzles and Anomalies," p. 18.
32. For a detailed analysis of the issues surrounding school bureaucratization and conflict in this period see Katz, *Reconstructing American Education.* Also see Tyack, "School Governance in the United States: Historical Puzzles and Anomalies," and Bryk, et al., "High School Organization and Its Effects on Teachers and Students: An Interpretive Summary of the Research," in *Choice and Control in American Education*, vol. 1, ed. William H. Clune and John F. Witte (New York: Falmer Press, 1990).
33. Tyack, "School Governance in the United States: Historical Puzzles and Anomalies," p. 19.
34. Cuban, "Reforming Again, Again, and Again," p. 4. Also see Marie Wirsing, "A Sense of Courage," *Educational Studies*, vol. 10, no. 2 (Summer, 1979), pp. 147–161.
35. Joel Spring, *Conflict of Interest: The Politics of American Education* (New York: Longman Publishing Group, 1993), p. 61.
36. Tim L. Mazzoni, "The Changing Politics of State Education Policy Making: A Twenty-Year Minnesota Perspective," *Educational Evaluation and Policy Analysis*, vol. 15, no. 4. (1993), p. 357.
37. Katz, *Reconstructing American Education*, p. 111.
38. Tyack, "School Governance in the United States: Historical Puzzles and Anomalies," p. 21.

# 4

# FOUR SECTORS
# OF INFLUENCE

*What is really going on here?*
—Erving Goffman, 1974

Educational governance includes many more organizations and actors than those representing the public schools. Participants come from other public agencies, the private sector, universities, special interest groups, and the media. Governing bodies must deal with a wide variety of social, political, and economic issues. Local school administrators regularly negotiate with district, state, and federal officials in order to craft intergovernmental agreements. Advisory boards and accountability committees meet with teachers and administrators to make critical budget decisions. Governors and state legislators spend countless hours on regulatory questions that directly impact schools and classrooms. All of these governance discussions involve competing interests and complicated negotiations between many different organizations and individuals.

The diversity and increasing number of interest groups from all sectors of society can be overwhelming for anyone trying to bring about system-wide reforms. Change at one level within the educational system generally requires cooperation and support from other levels. In order to generate effective approaches to reform, a complete picture of the intergovernmental nature of the American system is needed. This chapter provides a roadmap through American education by identifying the structural components of governance from the local to the federal level.

## THE SIZE AND SCOPE OF PUBLIC EDUCATION IN THE UNITED STATES

Education is the largest civil enterprise, representing major economic, social, and cultural commitments. Public schools enroll 47.6 million students, employing 6.9 million people or more than 20 percent of the U.S. labor force.[1] Public education is big business when it is considered as a percentage of local, state, and national economies. Comparing education-related expenditures to health care spending in 1990, when Medicaid payments and support for health and hospitals are combined, the total health care expenditure still comprises less than half the amount states spent on elementary and secondary education.[2] State and local expenditures for education increased from about $108.4 billion a decade ago to around $279 billion in 1992–93. State spending for highways and corrections is also dwarfed by the state's contribution to school finance formulas. Viewed from a national context, the total expenditures for education amounted to 7.8 percent of the gross domestic product in 1992–93, a higher percentage than previous years. In 1990, the United States spent over 18 percent of all its government expenditures on education, compared to 15.1 percent in 1960.[3]

Politically, decision making is decentralized by the Constitution's delegation of authority over education to the states. With the exception of Hawaii, which has one school district, the states have further delegated a good share of decision making authority to local school districts, along with varying degrees of fiscal, managerial and curricular autonomy. There are approximately 14,700 school districts in the United States and 110,000 individual schools.[4]

The American educational system includes common governance structures superimposed upon a diversity of local governance practices. In a democratic and decentralized educational system, the practice of governance is shaped by small groups of people in thousands of locations. At the same time, state governments prescribe certain political structures and legal constraints that require a high degree of structural and procedural commonality. A societal commitment of this magnitude requires a governance system that is both representative of local community interests and consistent with democratic principles. The following description of four sectors of influence attempts to capture the detail and diversity in the American system.

## FOUR SECTORS OF GOVERNANCE

Public decisions are the outcomes of four different sectors of political influence: government, the private sector, nonprofit/special interest groups, and the media. These categories of formal authority are represented by both elected and appointed policy makers. Table 4.1 graphically depicts four sectors and their representatives.

This view of governance represents recent changes in American politics and the evolution of more complex approaches to public participation. Within this model, schools, administrators, and teachers represent the public, governmental sector of decision making. Citizens, parents, and students can be represented by more than one sector at the same

**TABLE 4.1    Four Sectors of Educational Governance**

| Four Sectors | Institutions/ Organizations | Participants— Elected | Participants— Appointed |
|---|---|---|---|
| Education as a Unit of Government | Local School Site School Districts State Agencies Federal Agencies and Programs | Boards Legislatures Governors Members of Congress | Superintendents Administrators City and State School Officers Program Directors Advisors Evaluators Federal Level Administrators Secretary of Education |
| Private Sector | Businesses Corporations Contractors Affiliations Service Providers (e. g., Utility and Franchise Companies) | | Representatives on Advisory Committees Site-Based Management Teams Consultants |
| Nonprofit and Special Interest Groups | Professional Affiliations Single Issue Groups Coalitions Foundations (e.g., PTA, NEA, AFT, AASA) | | Administrators Lobbyists Staff Advisors Experts |
| Media as Information Brokers and Gatekeepers | Television Newspapers Radio Electronic News Publishers | | Reporters Public Relations Officers Editorialists Media Representatives |

time. For example, a parent may be a member of the local Parent Teacher Association (PTA), a nonprofit, special interest organization. That same person may also be a teacher and member of a teacher union that acts as a special interest. Citizens have increasingly relied on one or more of these groups instead of direct, personal involvement in school or system-wide policy making. Four sectors provide multiple opportunities for participation and representation, but they also add to the complexity of the political process.

A multi-sector view of participation in governance is a significant departure from the idea that American politics is based on one person-one vote and representative democracy. Despite the ideals of individualism and democracy, the American political system is largely based upon political interaction among associations of individuals rather than individual citizens. Long ago, observers saw that few ordinary citizens have access to the actual workings of policy making. These conditions led to the development of pluralism and group theories in American politics.[5]

Frequent overlap and conflict occur between the goals and interests of four sectors. There is some concern about the degree to which representatives from these groups accurately reflect the views of their constituents. However, at least four types of political interest are generally present in governance settings.

## Public Education as the Government Sector

Schools, districts, and state education agencies are units of government, legally, administratively, and politically. They are supported by public taxes and governed by the principles of representative democracy. Schools are the most numerous units of local government and they are increasingly tied to other public sector agencies through intergovernmental partnerships. School district personnel, including teachers and administrators, are public sector employees with regulatory restraints similar to other public sector workers. In most states and school districts, educators are eligible to participate in public employee benefits programs, including credit unions and pension funds. As organizations, school sites, and districts are considered components of the public sector regarding federal rules and regulations, tax status, and legal procedures.

Identifying educators as public sector representatives in governance has become an unpopular distinction. The growing distrust of government lessens the degree to which educators acknowledge schools as *government* or the public sector. As Chapter 6 points out, reformers advocating *schools of choice* believe that the public, governmental nature of education is the root of the problem, creating bureaucratic and inflexible environments. Despite these concerns, the nation's 14,700 school districts are still units of government and governed through public, democratic structures.

## The Private Sector's Role in Educational Governance

Businesses and corporations are involved in school systems in a variety of contexts. As suppliers of products and services—from textbooks to architectural designs—the private sector affects educational decisions in important but politically indirect ways. As a direct participant in governance, private sector involvement includes business executives on state and local accountability committees, advisory boards, and other ad hoc groups. Corporations and small business also sponsor programs and initiatives such as *adopt a school*, that create a context for direct participation in school-related decision making. At the national level, private sector groups with organized and ongoing efforts to influence educational decisions include the Committee for Economic Development, National Alliance of Business, the U.S. Chamber of Commerce, the Business Roundtable, National Association of Manufacturers, the Conference Board, and the American Business Conference.[6]

Private sector involvement in education has increased dramatically in the last ten years with the advent of state and national level reforms designed to make American education more competitive with school systems in other industrialized nations. The influence of private sector organizations and coalitions in educational decision making has increased as a function of state and national school reforms, which were largely the product of committees and advisory boards with strong private sector membership. Research suggests the business community is over-represented, in relation to the other three sectors, by its multiple forms of influence and by sophisticated pressure groups that outstrip the capacity of unpopular and underfunded public sector organizations.[7]

## Nonprofit and Special Interest Groups

The involvement of nonprofit organizations and special interest groups in education is representative of changes in the American political system in the last two decades. Governance is now more reliant on negotiations between special-interest groups, politicians, and government administrators.

Distinctions can be made between nonprofit and special interest organizations. In regard to participation in governance, both terms refer to organizations and individuals who operate separately from the public sector and are fundamentally designed to promote or influence a particular issue or agenda. Special interest groups are distinctly different from government because they are *private* associations whose main purpose is lobbying government to secure their own private ends. "The interest group is a vehicle through which individuals of like circumstances or convictions can collectively develop a position on an important issue and then bring influence to bear upon governmental policy making."[8] There is a blurring of roles between and among special interest groups and nonprofit organizations; but for purposes of a clarification of the structural components of governance, special interest groups and nonprofit organizations are used synonymously to represent a separate, third sector.

In the American context, interest groups reaffirm democratic governance by asserting that multiple and competing groups will preserve democratic values. James Madison argued in the *Federalist Papers* that power should be spread not only among agencies of government, but among interest groups that pressure government as "the building blocks of American politics."[9] The goal of pluralism in the expansive period of American government was to create new forums and opportunities for groups of citizens to participate in representative democracy. The idea was to encourage people to organize themselves into identifiable interest groups whose claims and aspirations the government could address. This approach evolved over time to allow the creation of thousands of public, private, and nonprofit organizations. Each group has a specific agenda and a related constituency. Political scientists have documented how interest groups form around issues and policies including health care, the environment, and education.

Pluralism is responsible for what has been described as a bargaining mode of governance. The highly organized and specialized qualities of nonprofit advocacy groups, political action committees, lobbyists, and privately funded think tanks have complicated the original meaning of pluralistic democracy. Opinions about the effects of the evolution of pluralism and interest group politics are mixed. On the positive side, interest groups are often the first to identify issues and formulate policy options. They produce a wealth of specialized information and knowledge beyond the capabilities of government agencies. Interest groups frequently work collaboratively to generate and sustain important public initiatives that are beyond the scope and capacity of public agencies.

Interest groups have come to be known as pressure groups, criticized for creating political gridlock in Washington. Studies of pressure group politics reveal many other problems.[10] Not all citizens and interests are evenly represented. Pressure-group politics favors financially strong private interests that can support the costs of lobbying, organizing, and documenting positions supporting narrow interests. Public officials can only act as referees or intermediaries, and the public interest becomes a confusing amalgamation and reconciliation of competing private interests.

Studies of the effects of interest groups in public education are also divided. There is wide agreement that interest group politics is present in educational governance. Educators are increasingly treated by political decision makers and often see themselves as one among many political interests. Some reformers believe that educators are not to be trusted, any more than any other parochial special interest group.[11] The view of educators as a special interest is reinforced in the idea of a "public school lobby," composed of organized groups of school boards, superintendents, teacher organizations, and parent-teacher associations who "have a stake in preserving and extending the quasi-monopoly that has been created."[12] Joel Spring describes how the "big three" special interest groups in education (foundations, teachers' unions, and the corporate sector) dominate educational governance at every level.[13]

These interpretations are largely based on policy conflicts at the state and federal level. They suggest that special interests in education are divisive and largely to blame for the slow pace of school reform. At the community level, interest group politics has been viewed in more positive terms. McCarty and Ramsey's influential classifications of community power structures depicts the pluralistic community as the ideal structure, in which no single group dominates the decision-making process, and competition represents broad community interest in the schools.[14] They argue that pluralistic communities are typically open-minded and rely on facts. However, there is some question whether this view of constructive pluralism can occur outside of stable and homogeneous communities. Even in stable suburban districts, special interests can redefine how the local governance process works. In recent years, there is growing concern that administrators are threatened and immobilized by well organized interests, such as taxpayer revolts, religious groups, and teachers' unions. Pressure groups often focus on single issues, ranging from school prayer to the inclusion of specific courses in the curriculum.

A representative and widely known example of an interest group in education is the Parent Teachers Association (PTA). This organization continues to be the largest volunteer group in the United States, and like other large associations, the PTA reflects the structure of three levels of governance, with a national office at the federal level, fifty branch offices representative of the fifty states, and over 30,000 units at the local level.[15] Other examples of nonprofit organizations and special interests, involved in governance from the local to national level include teachers' unions and organizations such as American School Board Association and the American Association of School Administrators. According to

Campbell: "The thousands of national interest groups are buttressed by fifty times that number of local, state, and regional branches, chapters, or other subunits. Almost without exception, interest groups come to have local, state, and national expressions and each group comes to represent an organizational network. . . . Major national groups like the U.S. Chamber of Commerce and the American Federation of Labor operate quite effectively through such local-state-national networks."[16]

## *The Media's Role in Educational Governance*

Media organizations participate in governance through their unique role as information brokers. The media is present at the local level through newspaper, radio, and television coverage. Reporters and journalists are influential yet indirect participants in governance. At the state and federal levels, media organizations play a significant role in choosing the news that will be reported, while making "news" through analyses and editorial opinions about educational policies and programs. Public opinion is a critical factor in governance, and in an information age, public perceptions are gauged by surveys and polls conducted and/or interpreted by media-based organizations.

The influence of the media in educational governance can be seen in the complex interrelationships between information, organizations, and the acquisition of knowledge. Joel Spring defines information *gatekeepers* as: "individuals and organizations that influence the distribution of research and new knowledge."[17] The press is a primary gatekeeper, moving information from its specialized sources to the general public, who make decisions based on the level of content, style, and tenor of information that they receive.[18] Public relations directors and information officers in school districts are also gatekeepers, often playing critical roles in determining how, when and whether governance decisions will be communicated.

The power of the media can be examined from the perspective of the diversified activities of communications companies. Moffett reports that communications companies represent the consolidation of newspapers, magazines, movies, textbook and trade books, and other media. "As profit corporations, they (publishers) have far greater power to limit what I can read than any special-interest group."[19] Rapid developments in information technology and computer networks blur past distinctions between media organizations and suppliers of education-related information. The close connection between knowledge, information, education and the communications industry underscores the importance of the media in educational politics and decision making.

The role of the media in governance may become more important as market-based reforms gain in popularity. If schools compete for enrollments, they will increasingly rely on the media to communicate their philosophies and designs. Despite the continuous presence of the media in educational governance, there are few studies of its influence on school politics. Little is known about the influence of the media on the public's perceptions about the quality of American schools, even though the public relies heavily on newspaper and television reporting for information and opinions.

## Balancing Four Sectors

The presence of four sectors in educational governance is a relatively new phenomenon. It is difficult to determine the degree of influence the four sectors exhibit in the cumulative record of educational decision making. And little research has been conducted on educational politics that takes into account the relationship between these four sectors. There are concerns about the growing influence of special interest groups and the private sector in education, particularly in times of scarce public resources and lack of trust in government. Moffett states: "Profit corporations . . . now enjoy, along with various religious and secular factions, the powers of tyranny formerly reserved to government. Corporations are the most powerful part of the private sector because government has neither the legal nor financial means to control them."[20] There are countervailing questions about governments' lack of effectiveness in sponsoring and governing education. Proposals and programs to privatize public school are increasing in size and scope. The presence of new players in governance from these four sectors has sometimes involved deliberate attempts to exclude other potential participants in the policy process, especially teachers and teacher educators.[21]

As educational governance is now structured, it is incumbent upon anyone who participates to recognize the presence of these four sectors. Attempts to organize more effective governance structures will need to consider how to achieve an equitable balance of representation among four sectors of values and interests.

## EDUCATIONAL GOVERNANCE AT THE LOCAL, STATE, AND FEDERAL LEVEL

Within the governmental sector, political authority in education is distributed between three levels of government. At the local level, school districts are the central organizational structure for providing elementary and secondary education. State governments are responsible for establishing state-wide policies, particularly school finance systems and taxation policies. The federal government occupies the third level in educational governance, as demonstrated by congressional policies and the administration of federal programs through the Department of Education.

In the wake of site-based management, political authority at the school site or building level has been categorized as a fourth level of educational governance.[22] However, building-level governance is still highly controlled and confined by the district structure. Recent studies of site-based management and decentralization show that most school-level groups still have limited legal and regulatory authority and are rarely involved in significant policy changes.[23] It is difficult to characterize governance at the school level because of the differences between school settings and the contextual nature of community politics. Another challenge to understanding governance at the school building level is the lack of research on the political dynamics within schools, contrasted with the literature on district-wide governance issues.

At each of these levels of authority, responsibility for the control and management of education is distributed among the three branches of government. As in other functions of government, this division of responsibility is purposefully designed to inhibit any one branch from dominating the others. The founders were particularly concerned that the executive branch could become as powerful as the monarchies of Europe. *Government* is often associated with the agencies, programs, and services of the executive branch; but the legislative and judicial branches are powerful forces in educational decision making. Table 4.2 lists three levels of government, three branches of government at each level, and their respective agencies and participants.

The separation of powers in the American political system between three functional branches of government is embedded in the design of public education. The executive branch is associated with the school district system and educational administration. Representative democracy and local control are manifested in the creation of local school boards, the equivalent of the legislative branch of government. The judicial branch oversees the implementation of the fundamental goal of providing equal educational opportunity for all students and the protection of the rights of individuals in schools as set forth in the Constitution.

There are overlaps of authority and responsibility between these three branches. For example, state and federal judges are often accused of *micro-managing* school districts by virtue of strict legal rulings that

**TABLE 4.2   Three Branches and Three Levels of Government**

| Three Levels of Government | Three Branches of Government | | |
| --- | --- | --- | --- |
| | Executive | Legislative | Judicial |
| *Local Government* | | | |
| Organization | Schools & District Systems | School Board | City/County Judicial System District Judicial Staff |
| Participants in Governance | Administrators Superintendents Teachers & Staff | School Board Members | Judges Attorneys Law Enforcement Officers District's Legal Staff |
| *State Government* | | | |
| Organization | Department of Education | State Board of Education State Legislature Legislative Committees | State Judicial System |
| Participants in Governance | Governors Chief State School Officers Department Staff | Board Members Legislators Elected State Superintendent | Judges State Attorney General & Staff Regulators |
| *Federal Government* | | | |
| Organization | U.S. Department of Education Education Related Agencies & Programs | U.S. Congress | U.S. Supreme Court Federal Judicial System |
| Participants in Governance | President Secretary of Education Administrators in Related Agencies | Members of Congress & Staff | U.S. Supreme Court Justices District Judges Judicial Personnel |

limit the authority of local level administrators. Questions about the efficiency of this design are discussed later in this chapter; but at the broad structural level of governance, it is important to acknowledge the presence of three branches of government at all levels of governance.

## Local Level Governance

School districts are the basic governmental unit through which local control of education is exercised. School districts are units of government, possessing quasi-corporate powers, created and empowered by state law to administer schools and systems. By tradition and practice, the roughly 15,000 local school districts build considerable variation in to American education, despite the growth of state and national authority in the last twenty years.[24]

Educational administrators represent the executive branch in local school governance. The district superintendent is generally appointed by the school board, although he or she is elected in some districts. Administrators are assigned positions and responsibilities in a process similar to bureaucratic procedures in other public agencies. Educational administrators are representative of the executive branch to the extent that they perform as executives, favoring a managerial approach to schools as organizations and the values of efficiency and specialization.

School boards represent the legislative branch of government at the local level. As with legislators at the state level, school boards value representativeness, responsiveness, and accountability to constituents. School boards play an important role in decisions about budgets, the general organization of school districts, teachers' union contracts, implementation of curricula, and personnel and student policies.

Judicial responsibilities within a school district are not as clearly defined or delegated to a particular group or individual. School boards and administrators retain considerable legal authority that is interpreted and adjudicated by attorneys and legal staff employed by districts. City and county judges and law enforcement agencies often participate in educational governance, even though they are separate from the school district system. Division of judicial authority within and outside of school districts helps explain the confusing and conflictive nature of many legally related governance decisions.

Within the context of *government*, school districts operate as complex systems of executive, legislative, and judicial authority. As organizations, districts are bureaucratic by design, with extensive legal controls and mandates. School board members, district administrators, and teachers play relatively well-defined roles, with predictable constraints and operating routines which are generally expressed in bureaucratic terms.[25] Governance authority shifts between different groups within this structure, depending on the issue in question and contextual factors within the district. For example, school board members in one district may delegate authority to a "strong superintendent," while in other districts the school board members may become directly involved in management decisions. Conversely, an elected superintendent represents a mix of the authorities of the executive and legislative branch combined.

## State Level Governance

State governance structures are designed to support, regulate, and evaluate the operation of local schools. State government is critical in educational governance due to Constitutional provisions that empower the states to establish school systems. Recent state-initiated school reforms underscore the importance of state-level authority.

All three branches of state government are involved in governing education, although there are differences between the states in the distribution of executive and legislative authority. The executive branch includes the governor, the chief state school officer (a generic term that includes state superintendents, state commissioners, and other titles) the state board of education, the staff of the state department of education and other state agencies.[26] However, in almost half of the states, chief state school officers are elected by popular vote, while in approximately half of the remaining states they are appointed by state boards of education, or in four states appointed by the governor.

State legislators embody the legislative branch of government and the political values of representativeness, responsiveness, and accountability to the citizenry. State legislatures have become more active and influential in relation to other levels and branches of government, so much so that they have been depicted as big school boards. Legislative subcommittees overseeing topics such as school finance and state-wide performance standards enact policies with the assistance of state agencies and special interest lobbyists that are not available to district level policy makers.

Representing the judicial branch, state court authority in governance has expanded, particularly in relation to desegregation decisions in the 1960s and school finance rulings in the 1970s. During the 1980s, state supreme courts found school finance systems unconstitutional in five states and by 1990, court cases had been filed or were planned in twenty-five states.[27] One example of how the influence of the judicial branch is exercised is in Kentucky. In 1989, the Kentucky Supreme Court ruled the entire system of school governance and finance to be in violation of the state constitution's requirement to provide an "efficient system of common schools." The General Assembly responded in 1990 by passing the Kentucky Education Reform Act, which fundamentally changes traditional governance structures along with providing additional resources for new educational programs and initiatives. The legislation is being implemented over a five year period by state and local administrators and elected officials. The judicial branch continues to monitor its implementation and eventual effectiveness within the context of the state's constitution.

Considering the combined effects of the three branches of government at the state level requires an analysis of policies and programs from a systems perspective. Because of the authority of the states under the U.S. Constitution and the recent emphasis on state-based reforms, state government is at the center of the action in governance. States define the scope of education, such as the existence of kindergarten, vocational education, and hours of instruction. State agencies define how different components of the educational system interact with one another, including enrollment policies and articulation agreements between public institutions. The legislature usually delegates to the state board of education the prerogative to set minimum standards for curriculum, student graduation requirements, and, in some instances, instructional materials. Some states adopt a standard course of study, or guidelines for subject areas, including the adoption of textbooks. Many states have created detailed statutes and state regulations governing teacher and administrator certification.

State level governance is perhaps the most visible and politically controversial in relation to school finance and taxation policies. The state's share of school funding has generally increased, while the local portion of tax revenues has declined or remained constant and the federal share has remained small. With states paying a larger share of educational services that are delivered through local districts, regulation and oversight of district spending and general performance have increased. The implications of the increasing authority of state government in public education are addressed in future chapters.

## Federal Level Governance

Within the context of formal responsibilities, the federal government maintains a limited role in education due to constitutional provisions that delegate authority to lower levels of government. Even with the growth of categorical aid programs and investments in research and curriculum development, the federal government contributes less than six percent of school operating budgets.[28] However, the federal government's influence on public education is much larger than its financial investment suggests. The influence of federal level policies is exercised through the administrative, political, and legal actions of powerful agencies. School principals will attest to the ubiquitous influence of the federal government in local schooling.

The executive branch at the federal level includes the President, the Secretary of Education, the Department of Education, and the many research-related agencies sponsored by other departments in the federal government. The legislative branch is represented by the members of Congress, their immediate staff, and Congressional research agencies. Political authority is interconnected and interdependent between the executive and legislative branches, as federal agencies administer programs and policies created by the legislative branch. Federal resources for education range from curriculum development grants sponsored by the National Science Foundation to training programs administered by the Department of Labor. Congressional legislation such as the Elementary and Secondary Education Act includes funding for a variety of programs, particularly for low-income families.

One highly publicized example of how the federal level of government affects education is the establishment of national goals for public schools. Both Republican and Democratic presidents have joined forces with state policy makers to recommend national goals and curriculum standards for state and local school systems.[29] Beyond the merits or issues of the goals themselves is the shift of governance authority to higher and more centralized levels of governmental authority.

The federal role in educational governance has also expanded through the authority of the judicial branch. Since desegregation decisions in the 1950s and the enforcement of civil rights rulings in the 1960s, the courts have exercised greater authority in public education. The influence of the federal judiciary continued through the last two decades in relation to Supreme Court rulings affecting the rights of students, parents, teachers, and administrators. Federal policies such as The Americans with Disabilities Act (ADA) require local compliance that involves both legal and administrative considerations.

## IMPLICATIONS OF THREE LEVELS AND THREE BRANCHES OF GOVERNMENT

The distribution of political authority among three levels of government creates both opportunities and issues. As a decentralized system, it provides freedom for state and local governments to pursue a diversity of approaches to education. The existence of 15,000 school districts and lay boards represents points of access for citizen involvement, both through formal elected office and informal input at school board meetings. Individual schools, teachers, and curricula can be responsive to community interests. Most industrialized nations have more centralized and uniform educational systems in which decisions are made at a national level and local level participation in decision making is limited.

The American governance structure has also been depicted as fragmented, bureaucratic, and ineffective.[30] The existence of several layers of political authority gives rise to conflict, competition, and contradictory policies that ebb and flow between levels of government. Increased state and federal involvement in school reform has at times been at cross purposes with the goals of local school boards and administrators. Kenneth Wong observed that functional and jurisdictional fragmentation among the three levels of government is largely responsible for inequities in educational resources. He studied three different policies designed to achieve educational equity and concluded:

> *Specifically, federal policy has focused on special-needs populations but has paid limited attention to territorial disparity with states. States' territorial strategies are designed to equalize inter-district fiscal capacity but are largely quiescent on how state aid should be used to address the needs of disadvantaged students in declining neighborhood schools. Local distributive policies not only fail to consider differential needs among student groups within the district but, with their focus on personnel allocation, widen the gap between declining and stable neighborhood schools. Together, the three sets of equity policies have largely failed to close the resource gap between rich and poor districts and, within districts, between schools in stable neighborhoods and those in poor neighborhoods.*[31]

Studies of federalism and intergovernmental relations also document fragmentation, duplication, and incoherence between levels of government and educational policies. Chapter 6 describes the inherent contradictions between decentralization reforms that emphasize local control as opposed to centralized reforms designed to establish national standards and uniform goals.

## The Problems of Bureaucratic Governance

Reformers and a growing number of citizens believe that the problems in elementary and secondary education are created by *government bureaucracy, federal regulations, the courts, politicians, and state interference.* These frustrations often derive from the separation of powers and the fundamental structure of American governance. Comprehensive studies of public schools as organizations conclude that public education has become too bureaucratic, rule-bound, and inefficient.[32]

Social scientists have produced a long list of bureaucratic pathologies. Bureaucracy demands a high level of conformity, reinforced through personnel rules and managerial reward structures. Preoccupation with formal authority works against individual creativity and collective interest. Neutrality and impartiality carried to the extreme create a general sense of impersonality. Specialization often inhibits system-wide communications and leads bureaucrats to lose sight of the overall goals and objectives of the organization. Specialized units in bureaucracies become insulated and avoid negative feedback.

Bureaucratic rationality and control were combined with scientific management in order to design schools as efficient organizations. The "school as a factory" metaphor was used in the 1930s as a positive model to guide educators. However, it was not long before the dysfunctional aspects of bureaucracies were identified in many school systems. Urban schools were criticized for becoming complex structures that allowed school officials to operate autonomously from the influence of the community. Decades of research document the problem of teachers becoming isolated from one another by narrowly defined specialties. Students are divided and separated by grade levels and subject areas.[33] Schools as bureaucracies have been renounced for sacrificing freedom and creativity in favor of control. Administrators, teachers, and students have described the oppressive and authoritarian attitudes that pervade highly structured, factory-like environments.

The term "bureaucratic" has become synonymous with waste and government inefficiency. Bureaucratic educational systems are associated with fragmented and disjointed governance authority. Political authority at the federal, state, and local levels was intentionally dispersed as a reflection of mistrust in centralized government. However, decentralization requires the creation of multiple levels of government. Over time, the interrelationships between different levels in educational policy making have become complicated and ineffective. The states depend on localities for policy execution, as any higher-level agent depends on lower-level implementation structures. State governments should be constrained by what localities will accept, yet the states often act independently. Similarly, the federal government has only a modest constitutional role in education. Yet federal agencies have pushed dramatic initiatives designed to change state and local education policy. Even though governmental levels reflect a hierarchical structure, agencies throughout the system retain much of their operating independence.[34]

The resulting governance process has been depicted as incoherent and redundant. Organizational patterns in education are described as loosely coupled, disjointed, attenuated, and generally ineffective. School reformers are concerned that the net effect of bureaucratic governance is a system that is highly resistant to any kind of change. School bureaucracies have become intractable institutions, able to avoid, ignore, and resist major reform efforts.

One of the more controversial criticisms of schools as bureaucracies is the presumed link between democratic control and bureaucratic organization. Chubb and Moe's *Politics, Markets, and America's Schools*, argued that "institutions of direct democratic control promote ineffective school organizations. Driven by politics, these institutions encourage the bureaucratization and centralization of school control."[35] Throughout their arguments supporting schools of choice and market-based reform, Chubb and Moe conclude that organizational structure is *the* problem: "Its bureaucracy problem is not that the system is bureaucratic at all, but that it is too heavily bureaucratic—too hierarchical, too rule-bound, too formalistic—to allow for the kind of autonomy and professionalism schools need if they are to perform well."[36] They further argue that the uncertainty of democratic policies causes educational leaders to construct bureaucracies as a means of control and protection.

These authors are not the first to raise the issue of the relationship between democratic governance and the creation of bureaucratic institutions. Educational historians note that "liberals and conservatives have attacked bureaucracy as a major source of problems in education. The radical right argued in the 1950s that the educational bureaucracy made the schools havens for communist thinking by introducing progressive education. . . . On the other hand, in the 1960s, liberals attacked urban educational bureaucracies for promoting racism, segregation, and social class discrimination."[37]

The assumption that democratic government inevitably produces bureaucratic organizations can be challenged. Scholars in public administration note there are conflicts between democracy and bureaucracy:

> *Democracy presumes plurality and diversity, while bureaucracy requires unity. Dispersion of power and equal access are essential to democracy, while bureaucracy demands a hierarchy of authority. Command and control are integral to bureaucracy, but democracy requires liberty and freedom. Officials of bureaucracy are appointed and enjoy long tenure, while democracy means election of officials with relatively short terms and potentially frequent turnover. In democracy, everyone is to have the opportunity to participate in the process, whereas in bureaucracy, participation is limited by where one fits in the hierarchy of authority. Finally, democracy cannot exist without openness, while bureaucracy thrives with secrecy and control over information.*[38]

One could argue whether there are cause and effect relationships between a democratic governance system and the bureaucratization of public agencies. There is considerable evidence to suggest the problems associated with bureaucracy are more the result of scientific management principles that have created large school districts and complicated administrative practices.

Criticisms based solely on levels of efficiency and organizational complexity overlook other important considerations of the goals and structure of American education. Rosenbloom's research on the administrative implications of the separation of powers helps explain why educational governance is inefficient by design:

> As Justice Brandeis pointed out, the founder's purpose in creating the constitutional branches was not simply to facilitate efficiency, coordination, and a smooth functioning of government generally. The purpose was also to create a system that would give each branch a motive and a means for preventing abuses or misguided action by another. This would prevent the "accumulation of all powers, legislative, executive, and judiciary, in the same hands," which, as Madison wrote in Federalist #47, the founders considered to be "the very definition of tyranny." But the separation of powers would also create a tendency toward inaction. Not only would each branch check the others, but a system of checks and balances would also serve as a check on popular political passions.[39]

The legal authority of the judicial branch was necessary for the desegregation of public education in the 1950s, despite decades of progressive reforms that placed greater trust in *professional* school executives. State systems of school finance, formulated by the legislative branch, are designed to reduce inequities between local school districts. Historically, the presence of three levels and three branches of government has often been a critical factor in building and maintaining America's system of free and legally protected public schools.

It is clear that both democratic governance and bureaucratic structures will continue to exist in public education. The way educational governance works in the future depends on how administrators and policy makers balance the effects of bureaucratic structures with democratic governance. Reforms emphasizing site-based management, for example, can be creative ways to retain democratic decision making while reducing the negative aspects of large, bureaucratic school systems.

## CONSIDERATIONS FOR STRUCTURAL REFORM

As with other aspects of educational governance, the formal structures of school boards, districts, state agencies and federal policies are undergoing careful scrutiny in the 1990s. Many of the proposals to privatize public schools and expand school choice are attempts to emulate the organizational and political structures in private schools. Many structural reforms are deceptively simple, suggesting there are objective and technical ways to modify a system that is in fact highly politicized and resistant to change. Changing formal governance structures requires the support of the public through democratic participation.

Outside the formal domain of elected officials and government's role in *governance* are the political dynamics brought about by the private sector, special interest groups, and the media. The increasing influence of these groups is often demonstrated in the form of policy *networks*, composed of issue-specific experts and influential actors from one or more of the four sectors working together on a particular issue. Researchers can only begin to map the actions of these networks before they disperse and reassemble around a new issue or initiative. Recent studies demonstrate how policy networks have become powerful agents in relation to the formal branches and levels of government.[40]

The existence of four sectors in governance, combined with the presence of multiple levels and branches of government, suggests changes in structures will be difficult to achieve. However, change is possible if not probable, given developments in other sectors of society and the widespread demand for educational reform. The following list of considerations for structural reform is designed to support change by clarifying the nature and breadth of the challenge.

1. Structural problems are not restricted to one level of educational governance.

There is plenty of evidence to conclude that the entire, multi-leveled structure of governance needs to be improved, modified, and/or fundamentally changed. Observers of past reforms have documented ways in which political authority shifts back and forth between existing levels of governance without any real effects on schools and student performance. It is becoming more apparent that changes must take into account the interconnected and interdependent nature of educational governance.

At the local level, the Institute for Educational Leadership's extensive studies of school boards conclude that the structure and operations of school boards are "not sufficient to meet new challenges of the external environment around schools."[41] In the 1990s, local boards are being pulled apart by supporters of site-based management on one side and state and federal reforms and mandates on the other. State authorities (legislators, governors, and chief state school officers) have increased their influence over funding and policy from the top. Simultaneously, employee unions, parents, interest groups, and private agencies have squeezed the discretionary zone of school board control from the bottom.

There are serious structural issues at the state and federal levels of governance. Many of the rules, regulations, and inter-agency agreements established by state agencies have not changed since the 1940s, despite the activism of the states in school reform in the last decade.[42] The role of the federal government in education has been uneven. Federal funding has fluctuated with changes in the presidency and Congress and is constrained by economic and ideological factors. Recent governance studies document the shift in control and financing of education to the state and federal levels, even though it may contribute to a larger problem of intergovernmentalism, in which more levels of government are responsible for more programs and policies. However, "common sense says that when all (levels of government) are nominally responsible, none is truly responsible."[43]

Beyond the issues of formal governmental authority are concerns about the growing influence of the nongovernmental sectors in educational policy and governance. The multi-sector model described earlier is a relatively new phenomenon in American politics, and there is little evidence that the presence of new actors in governance has been widely acknowledged, accepted, or even understood.

**2. A public education system requires a democratic governance structure.**

Reformers must be sensitive to the public and democratic nature of elementary and secondary education. Efficiency oriented reforms that emphasize managerial and organizational models from the private sector overlook the fundamental goals of equal educational opportunity and democratic participation in the governance of American education. There is little doubt that a political system of checks and balances between the three branches of government has created problems, complexities, and inefficiencies. However, it has also supported the creation of the most comprehensive and diverse educational system in the world. American education is built on two fundamental structures; it is tax supported, and it is controlled through lay governance. As long as these two structures are in place, governance must be organized in certain public ways.

Accepting and building a *public* and democratic educational system require the ability to distribute and share political power. A multi-sector model of governance requires all participants to think comprehensively and publicly. As Cremin states: "By thinking *publicly*, I mean several things. To begin, it means we must be aware that public thinking about education and public policy making for education goes on at a variety of levels and in a variety of places. It goes forward at the local, state, regional, federal, and international levels, and it proceeds in legislatures, in the courts, in executive agencies, and in private and quasi-public civic organizations."[44] There are many profound and difficult challenges inherent in thinking and managing *publicly*, not the least of which is to determine who is the *public* and what is in the *public interest*.

One of the first challenges in reforming educational governance is to understand its complex, intergovernmental qualities. The reason that the role of government in education is so difficult to appreciate fully is that in very basic ways it does not vary from one public school to the next. All public schools are governed by democratic institutions of the same basic form at the local level and then organized into larger systems of schools governed by institutions, again of the same basic form, at the state level. All of these systems are then subject to the influence and control of one set of democratic institutions at the national level.[45] These attributes require an ability to appreciate and work within high levels of organizational complexity and political uncertainty.

**3.** A complex, multi-leveled, public system will be difficult to change.

America's multi-sectored, multi-leveled governance model evolved over many years through the action of countless agencies and individuals. Any significant structural change must take into account many political and organizational factors. Public agencies are vulnerable to stalemate; they are especially good at blocking and frustrating attempts at change.[46] There are vested interests at different levels of authority who oppose changes that limit their power. Institutional barriers to change must be considered, such as the historical patterns of decision making and exclusive political cultures that have become insular and institutionalized.

Structural changes can rarely occur at one level of governance without the involvement of another level of authority. Cohen and Spillane observed:

> *The flood of state and federal policies and programs coursed through a large and loosely jointed governance system, yet agencies throughout the system have retained much of their independence. For instance, the states depend on localities for political support and policy execution, as any higher level agent depends on subordinates. State governments, therefore, should be constrained by what localities will accept, yet the states often act with remarkable independence. . . . Similarly, the national government has only a modest constitutional role in education, and it has long deferred to state and local governments.*[47]

Reforms must take into account the partitioned and defended bases of political authority at each level in the educational system. It becomes apparent why many reforms fail and why completely different structures are being proposed.

**4.** There is little agreement over the direction of structural reform.

Views of a better governance structure vary widely, just as the definitions of the problems of governance reflect different political and philosophical perspectives. Public education is described both as a uniform monopoly and as a loosely defined and highly decentralized system. Each of these views logically lead to different conclusions about the direction and shape of governance changes. Reforms in the 1990s range from greater centralization with an expanded state and federal role to greater decentralization and increased local control. Many believe that the democratic nature of governance has led to a bureaucratic and politicized system that lies at the heart of the problem. Other reformers and scholars have focused on organizational issues and the problems brought about by tightly controlled, scientific management principles that are ill suited to the uncertain, social and political environments of schools. There are calls for greater flexibility and adaptability along with proposals to more tightly couple institutions and levels of government.

The resulting contradictions and contrasts suggest that the direction of structural reforms will remain unclear for some time. It will be important for reformers and citizens alike to remember that there may be no "one best" governance structure and that changes will need to take into account the multiple goals of American education.

5. Structural reforms need to consider impacts on teaching and learning in schools.

Considerable disagreement and controversy exist in the research community about the effects of governance on teaching and learning. Research supporting structural reforms has generally been disconnected from classroom instruction and student learning. Thus, it has been difficult to establish direct causal links between governance factors and student-teacher performance. There is evidence that structural reforms have purposefully excluded the involvement and input of educators.

On the other hand, there are numerous studies demonstrating the importance of governance structures on the organization and environment of schools. The research of effective schools shows that quality teaching and learning depend on several factors that must be considered simultaneously, including governance structures.[48] Studies of school cultures show how authority patterns between teachers and administrators affect teacher morale and the learning environment.

Aside from specific research findings, students inevitably learn about government by observing governance in practice in schools. Students and teachers are the eventual focus of governance decisions and even though political factors may be subtle or covert, they are part of the environment of schools. As future citizens, students experience authority and democracy in school settings, while learning about policies and politics in school buildings and districts.

6. Improving educational governance structures is critical in a democratic society.

The structure of educational governance is important to other public and private institutions outside of schools and educational agencies. The way public education functions is a significant reflection of public values in the United States; and because of the relatively large size of education in relation to all other public investments, and the local nature of education, the way in which governance is organized and how it operates are serious social and political issues.

## SUMMARY

Governance is composed of many different agencies, actors, and interests. Four sectors of governance operate at three different levels of government. Politically, decision making is decentralized by the Constitution's delegation of authority over education to the states. As a consequence, the structure of the institutions and the procedures for governing schools are complex, multi-dimensional, and representative of many different interests and ideologies.

Schools, districts, and state education agencies are units of government, legally, administratively, and politically. As organizations, school sites and districts are considered components of the public sector regarding federal rules and regulations, tax status, and legal procedures. Businesses and corporations are involved in educational systems in a variety of ways. As a direct participant in governance, private sector involvement includes business executives on state and local accountability committees, advisory boards, and other ad hoc groups. The influence of private sector organizations and coalitions in educational decision making has increased as a function of state and national school reforms, which were largely the product of committees and advisory boards with strong private sector membership. The involvement of nonprofit organizations and special interest groups in education is representative of changes in the American political system that have occurred in the last two decades. The extent to which schools benefit from interest groups is highly dependent on the ability of administrators to create a forum and a context to incorporate constructive demands. Media organizations participate in governance through their unique role as information brokers.

The separation of powers in the American political system between three functional branches of government is embedded in the design of public education. School districts are the basic governmental unit through which local control of education is exercised. State government is a critical level in educational governance due to Constitutional provisions that empower the states to establish school systems. The federal government maintains a limited role in education.

The American governance structure has been depicted as fragmented, bureaucratic, and ineffective. Formal organizational structures are the targets of reform in the 1990s. The existence of four sectors in governance, combined with the presence of multiple levels and branches of government, suggests changes in structures will be difficult to achieve. However, change is probable, given the widespread demand for school reform.

## SEMINAR QUESTIONS

1. Do you think the current structure of educational governance is functioning well enough to be retained?

2. If you were to make significant changes in the structure of educational governance, would you promote centralization or decentralization?

3. How would you describe the relationship between bureaucracy and democracy?

4. Would you sacrifice some of the decision making rules and procedures that promote democratic participation for a smoother-running governance system?

## SUGGESTED READINGS

Chubb, John E., and Terry M. Moe. *Politics, Markets, and America's Schools.* Washington, DC: Brookings, 1991.

Dye, Thomas R. *American Federalism: Competition Among Governments.* Lexington: Lexington Books, 1990.

Fuhrman, Susan H., ed. *Designing Coherent Education Policy.* San Francisco: Jossey-Bass, Inc., 1993.

Lowi, Theodore J. *The End of Liberalism: The Second Republic of the United States.* New York: Norton, 1979.

Rosenbloom, David. *Public Administration: Understanding Management, Politics and Law in the Public Sector.* New York: Random House, 1986.

# ENDNOTES

1. *Digest of Education Statistics* (Washington, DC: National Center for Educational Statistics, 1993). Also see Austin D. Swanson and Richard A. King, *School Finance: Its Economics and Politics* (New York: Longman, 1991), pp. 3–4.
2. Steven D. Gold, "One Approach to Tracking State and Local Health Spending," *Health Affairs* (1992), p. 4. Also see Julie Rovner, "Cost of Medicaid Puts States in Tightening Budget Vise," *Congressional Quarterly* vol. 49 (1991), p. 20.
3. National Center for Educational Statistics, *Digest of Educational Statistics*, (U.S. Department of Education: Washington, DC, 1993). Also see John Augenblick, et al., *How Much Are Schools Spending?* (Denver: Education Commission of the States, April 1993), p. iv.
4. U.S. Bureau of the Census (1988). Also see Austin D. Swanson and Richard A. King, *School Finance: Its Economics and Politics* (New York: Longman, 1991).
5. N. Joseph Cayer and Louis F. Weschler, *Public Administration: Social Change and Adaptive Management* (New York: St. Martin's Press, 1988), p. 23. This book draws on the work of Harold Lasswell and Daniel Lerner, *The Comparative Study of Elites* (Palo Alto, Calif.: Stanford University Press, 1952).
6. Jacqueline P. Danzberger, Michael W. Kirst, and Michael D. Usdan, *Governing Public Schools: New Times New Requirements* (Washington, DC: Institute for Educational Leadership, 1992), pp. 5–6.
7. James Moffett, *Harmonic Learning* (Portsmouth, NH: Boynton/Cook Publishers, 1992). Also see *The Bias of Pluralism*, ed. William E. Connolly (New York: Atherton, 1969).
8. Roald F. Campbell, et al., *The Organization and Control of American Schools* (Columbus, Ohio: Charles E. Merrill Publishing Co., 1980), p. 372.
9. Cayer and Weschler, *Public Administration: Social Change and Adaptive Management*.
10. Robert B. Reich, "Policy Making in a Democracy," in *The Power of Public Ideas*, ed. Robert B. Reich (Cambridge, Mass.: Ballinger Publishing, 1988). Also see Theodore J. Lowi, *The End of Liberalism: The Second Republic of the United States* (New York: Norton, 1979).
11. Richard F. Elmore, "School Decentralization: Who Gains? Who Loses?" in *Decentralization and School Improvement*, eds. Jane Hannaway and Martin Carnoy (San Francisco: Jossey-Bass, 1993), p. 39.
12. Paul Peterson, "Monopoly and Competition in American Education," in *Choice and Control in American Education*, vol. 1, eds. William H. Clune and John F. Witte (New York: Falmer Press, 1990), pp. 71–72.
13. Joel Spring, *Conflict of Interest: The Politics of American Education* (New York: Longman Publishing Group, 1993).
14. Donald McCarty and Charles Ramsey, *The School Managers: Power and Conflict in American Public Education* (Westport, Conn.: Greenwood, 1971).
15. Campbell, et al., *The Organization and Control of American Schools*, p. 326.
16. Campbell, et al., *The Organization and Control of American Schools*, p. 374.

17. Spring, *Conflict of Interests: The Politics of American Education*, p. 16.
18. Harlan Cleveland, *The Knowledge Executive* (New York: Truman Talley Books, 1985), p. 43.
19. Moffett, *Harmonic Learning*, p. 23.
20. Moffett, *Harmonic Learning*, pp. 27–28.
21. Hendrik D. Gideonse, "The Governance of Teacher Education and Systemic Reform," *Educational Policy*, vol. 7, no. 4 (December 1993), p. 396.
22. Swanson and King, *School Finance: Its Economics and Politics*, p. 48.
23. Priscilla Wohlstetter and Thomas M. Buffett "Promoting School-Based Management: Are Dollars Decentralized Too?" in *Rethinking School Finance: An Agenda for the 1990s*, ed. Allan R. Odden (San Francisco: Jossey-Bass, 1992), p. 159. Also see Elmore, "School Decentralization: Who Gains? Who Loses?" in *Decentralization and School Improvement*, pp. 44–45.
24. David K. Cohen and James P. Spillane, "Policy and Practice: The Relations Between Governance and Instruction," in *Designing Coherent Education Policy* (San Francisco: Jossey-Bass, Inc., 1993), pp. 35–95.
25. Richard F. Elmore, "Choice as an Instrument of Public Policy: Evidence from Education and Health Care," in *Choice and Control in American Education*, vol. 1, eds. William H. Clune and John F. Witte (New York: Falmer Press, 1990), p. 290.
26. Martha McCarthy, *State Education Governance Structures*, Education Commission of the States (Denver: November 1993).
27. Allen Odden, "School Finance and Education Reform: An Overview," in *Rethinking School Finance*, ed. Allen Odden (San Francisco: Jossey-Bass, Inc., 192), pp. 1–40.
28. David K. Cohen and James P. Spillane, "Policy and Practice: The Relations between Governance and Instruction," in *Designing Coherent Education Policy* (San Francisco: Jossey-Bass, Inc., 1993), pp. 35–95.
29. *America 2000: An Education Strategy* (Washington, DC: U.S. Department of Education, 1991). Also see *Mandate for Change*, eds. William Marshall and Martin Schram (Progressive Policy Institute: Barkley Books, 1993).
30. John Chubb, "Political Institutions and School Organization," p. 232. In *Choice and Control in American Education*, vol. 1, eds. William H. Clune and John F. Witte (New York: Falmer Press, 1990) pp. 227–234. Also see Cohen and Spillane, "Policy and Practice: The Relations Between Governance and Instruction," pp. 39–40.
31. Kenneth K. Wong, "Governance Structure, Resource Allocation, and Equity Policy," in *Review of Research in Education*, ed. Linda Darling Hammond. (Columbia University, New York: Teachers College, 1994), pp. 257–289.
32. Elmore, "School Decentralization: Who Gains? Who Loses?" in *Decentralization and School Improvement*, pp. 44–45.
33. Michael B. Katz, *Reconstructing American Education* (Cambridge, Mass.: Harvard University Press, 1987), p. 109.
34. Cohen and Spillane, "Policy and Practice: The Relations between Governance and Instruction," pp. 35–95. Also see Seymour B. Sarason, *The Case For Change: Rethinking the Preparation of Educators* (San Francisco: Jossey-Bass, 1993).
35. John E. Chubb and Terry M. Moe, *Politics, Markets, and America's Schools* (Washington, DC: Brookings, 1991), p. 146.
36. Ibid., p. 26.

37. Joel Spring, "Knowledge and Power in Research into the Politics of Urban Education," in *The Politics of Urban Education in the United States*, eds. James G. Cibulka, Rodney J. Reed and Kenneth K. Wong (Washington, DC: Falmer Press, 1991), p. 50.

38. Cayer and Weschler, *Public Administration: Social Change and Adaptive Management*, p. 15.

39. David Rosenbloom, *Public Administration: Understanding Management, Politics, and Law in the Public Sector* (New York: Random House, 1986), p. 224.

40. Cohen and Spillane, "Policy and Practice: The Relations Between Governance and Instruction," pp. 35–95. Also see Spring, *Conflict of Interests: The Politics of American Education.*

41. Danzberger, et al., *Governing Public Schools* (1992), p. 1.

42. Steven Porter, *Wisdoms Passing* (New York: Barclay House, 1989), p. 35.

43. Henry J. Walberg and Herbert J. Walberg III, "Losing Local Control," *Educational Researcher*, vol. 23, no. 5, (June–July 1994), p. 24.

44. Lawrence A. Cremin, "Public Education and the Education of the Public," in *History, Education, and Public Policy*, ed. Donald R. Warren (Berkeley, Calif.: McCutchan Publishing Corporation, 1978), pp. 30–31.

45. Chubb, "Political Institutions and School Organization," in *Choice and Control in American Education*, vol. 1, eds. William H. Clune and John F. Witte (New York: Falmer Press, 1990), p. 232. (pp. 227–234).

46. Elmore, "School Decentralization: Who Gains? Who Loses?" pp. 35–36.

47. Cohen and Spillane, "Policy and Practice: The Relations Between Governance and Instruction," pp. 35–95.

48. Joseph Blase, "Analysis and Discussion: Some Concluding Remarks," in *The Politics of Life in Schools*, ed. Joseph Blase (Newbury Park, Calif.: Sage Publications, 1991), p. 242. Also see Chubb and Moe, *Politics, Markets, and America's Schools*, p. 121.

# 5

# POLITICAL AND CULTURAL VALUES

*Education is a values battleground.*
—David Tyack

The interconnections between schools and communities open the governance environment to a multitude of political forces. As public institutions, schools are designed to reflect the demographics and social values of the communities they serve. They are affected by many of the same problems that are bringing about changes in American society: racial injustice, urban decay, poverty, scarcity of resources, misuse of political authority, and unemployment.[1] Cultural forces external to schools are multi-faceted, often interrelated, and inherently complex. They are difficult to directly observe, evaluate, or predict. Measures of public opinion about the quality of the schools, for example, are based on surveys and polls that are open to interpretation.

Despite the impressionistic and subjective qualities of community values, educators are directly affected by social and political forces outside of the schools. Being sensitive to environmental factors in, around, and far removed from school systems requires the use of information and insight from disciplines outside the field of education. Working with community interests also requires an acceptance of the value laden and political nature of public education. This chapter reviews many of the political and cultural forces that impact educational governance. The controversial and contradictory qualities of public values are explored in relation to educational policy making and administration.

Viewing the process of governance from a political perspective is a significant departure from legalistic and bureaucratic definitions of educational decision making. Bureaucratic organizations are by definition rational and logically organized to achieve predetermined goals. Authority to govern is formally allocated to elected officials and professional administrators. However, politics is not necessarily rational, orderly, or logical. The political approach views governance as the exchange of power between individuals and groups. Politics is about how people use power to influence others and protect themselves. The political perspective assumes there is conflict and competition among groups to achieve their ends; "It is about what people in all social settings think about and have strong feelings about, but what is so often unspoken and not easily observed."[2] Politics is driven by the immediacy of issues, conflicts, and attempts to resolve value differences.

The political aspects of education have received far less attention than issues related to structure and bureaucracy. Neither political scientists nor educators undertook a significant empirical study of the nature and effects of political factors in education during the entire first half of the twentieth century.[3] Existing studies of educational politics are more recent and less detailed than organizational research for several reasons. The progressive movement in the early twentieth century emphasized that all things political were to be kept out of the public schools. In educational administration, the principles of scientific management disavowed political considerations in the interests of efficiency and order. Combinations of these forces eliminated the legitimacy of ordinary political processes in education.

Events in the 1950s and 1960s dramatically increased interest in the political aspects of public schools and other public organizations. Educational politics escalated in the 1970s and 1980s as the school reform movement engaged state and federal political leaders. In the 1990s, administrators are becoming acutely aware that schools are political organizations, responding to many kinds of political questions. In many instances the schools have become the focal point of community politics. Public education has also become more politicized by the increased involvement of external interest groups.

## POLITICAL VALUES

The politics of education can be viewed within a values framework, in which trade-offs are considered and compromises are made in the pursuit of public values. Educational policy makers spend considerable time discussing and debating priorities that reflect social and political values. From this perspective, nationwide school reforms, as well as state and local educational policies are public records of value priorities and compromises.

Political values include more than partisan politics and the platforms of elected politicians. Democrats and Republicans often share the political values of liberty and equality, but hold widely differing views on how these values should be pursued. Vouchers and schools-of-choice proposals, for example, place liberty and freedom of choice as the highest priority among competing values. Political values have deeper meanings than partisan positions. Public values shape societies and build nations. The American Constitution, for example, is a statement of values and a unique record of compromises between political values.

Philosophers and educational theorists since Plato have known that education is a moral and value-laden enterprise.[4] Public education is deliberately value based in at least three dimensions. First, schools receive support through public taxes, which represent a formal and financial allocation of the public's *value* of education. Second, important policy decisions are made through a democratic process, which, as observers throughout history have noted, allows for and encourages competition and compromise among competing values. Third, teaching social values and transmitting an appreciation for a democratic culture is one of the foundations of public education.

Five values or objects of policy have been prominent in shaping the American educational system, each of which is rooted in political ideologies and philosophies of government[5]:

1. *Liberty*—The right to act in the manner of one's own choosing, not subject to undue restriction or control. Liberty is generally associated with the concept of private choice. The American federalists believed that good government is defined by its ability to preserve freedom of choice for its citizens. Choice is a difficult value to pursue through governmental action. It may be achieved more by inaction than positive policies. For example, greater choice may be provided in schooling by eliminating attendance policies and allowing families to choose among schools that may not reflect American values.

2. *Equality*—The state, ideal, or quality of being equal. Operational definitions of equality have come to include factors of condition, placing emphasis on the fairness of treatment. In the last two decades, equality has taken on connotations of equity. Equality and equity usually refer to civil rights and educational opportunity, not to personal characteristics and abilities. As a policy matter, equity is complicated. Policy makers cannot increase social equity, they can only create laws and programs that relieve the effects of inequality after it has been identified. Equality has been a central public value since the Declaration of Independence.

3. *Efficiency*—Defined in terms of classical economics, efficiency is determined by the ratio of inputs and outputs in the production of goods and

services. Efficiency as an organizational value is defined in terms of order, predictability, and control. In the educational lexicon, efficiency concerns are expressed in terms of accountability, standards, and other measures of quality and productivity. Educational administrators pursue efficiency in school operations by keeping costs down and graduation rates up.

4. *Community*—To value community is to seek a common bond that produces a sense of unity and nationhood. The Constitutional term for community is fraternity—a sense of national identity and a force for holding together a nation of immigrants. The value of community or fraternity is closely associated with the drive for common schools in the nineteenth century. The search for a sense of community amidst increasing diversity is a major challenge in the 1990s.

5. *Economic Growth*—Increasing the aggregate national production of goods and services. This political value involves the development of skills needed in the work force so the economy will expand at a desired pace. Scholars have also characterized economic growth as the means to pursue quality of life as a core value. Public policies supporting economic growth are designed to enhance the quality of life for citizens in a capitalistic, free market system.

The pursuit of five distinct values in education is a formidable task; and because of the conceptual inconsistencies among these values, public policies easily become contradictory or even counter-productive. The pursuit of equal educational opportunity usually decreases school efficiency. For example, a vote for standardizing curriculum materials may increase efficiency, but decrease freedom of choice and equity of access for special populations. Racial integration, for instance, advances the values of freedom and equality. However, integration policies usually entail busing, which increases transportation costs and decreases efficiency ratios. Governance becomes an exercise in finding a balance between competing values and political positions. Liberty, equality, efficiency, community, and economic productivity are at the core of most governance dialogues.

## Public and Private Values

Perhaps the most fundamental debate in educational governance is between the public and private values of schooling and the associated public and private forms of governance. Historians describe an inevitable tension in education because schooling occurs at the crossroads between the enhancement of individual autonomy and the demands of civilization and social order.[6] At the classroom and school level, educators must consider how to support independent thinking within the same environment that emphasizes cooperation, collaboration, and teamwork.

This same tension can be examined from a broader political perspective. Public values are directed at a sense of community, public interest, and civic involvement. Private values are associated with individual rights and private enterprise. These two broad sets of values have been debated throughout history and have long been at the center of political controversy. They also form the backdrop for the many waves and cycles of political reform.

Historian Arthur Schlesinger believes that American politics alternate at roughly thirty-year intervals between conservative periods that emphasize private values and liberal periods that promote public values. "The pattern of alternation can be seen as between times when private action, private enterprise, and private interest are deemed the best way to meet problems and times when the republic turns to public action and the public interest."[7] Public action takes shape in public programs and government services, including greater investments in public education. Private action in education translates as vouchers and the privatization of public schools.

This public-private dialectic is manifested in several additional governance debates. According to some reformers, private decisions will foster more variety and differentiation between schools and their academic offerings. Through the principles of supply and demand, good schools will thrive and poor schools will be eliminated. Public decision making represents the current system of governance, in which democratically elected school boards make decisions about schools and their offerings. The interests of the community as a whole are expressed through public policy and are determined in a group decision making context. Chapter 6 details the variety of ways public and private approaches to decision making are presented as school reforms.

## Partisan Political Values in Education

Many school reforms in the 1990s are associated with political parties and partisan politics. Just as the political dynamics of education intensified in the 1960s and 1970s, educational issues gained greater prominence in partisan political debates in the 1980s. Politicians took up the cause of school reform after the release of *A Nation at Risk*, which linked the quality of public education to the ability of American workers to compete in the international marketplace. Governors and state legislators gained visibility as they articulated their positions for or against specific approaches to improving schools. Political parties have followed with school reforms that reflect their value priorities and philosophies of government.

Partisan political influence is particularly evident at the federal level of government. In the 1980s, President Reagan's New Federalism initiatives attempted to curtail the authority of the federal government in public education. The Reagan administration consolidated and cut back federally funded programs in education. Upon his election, Reagan proposed to eliminate the U.S. Department of Education as a demonstration of the Republican Party's philosophy of reducing the size and scope of government. New Federalism policies succeeded in reducing the federal share of financial support for public education. During this period, the Democratic Party supported a stronger federal role in education, particularly through efforts to achieve equal educational opportunities and civil rights.

Presidents Reagan and Bush encouraged antigovernment sentiment and imposed a conservative philosophy of reliance on the private market to stimulate educational reform. Although the Department of Education was not eliminated, twelve years of Republican leadership changed the direction of federal educational policy.[8] The new language of reform in the 1980s reflected the Republican Party's views about the appropriate focus of educational policy. Excellence, ability, and productivity replaced the language of equity and access. Change in the language of school reform is summarized in Table 5.1.

The new language of federal educational policy stresses the link between educational attainment and economic productivity, which has gained visibility and support through the publication of several national reports sponsored by the private sector and business-oriented interest groups.

The 1984 and 1988 presidential campaigns, as well as scores of state and local elections, intensified partisan political divisions over school reform. The effectiveness of media campaigns on behalf of excellence, competition, and choice in education, directed by President Reagan, Secretary of Education William Bennett, and the Republican Party, are well documented.[10] In 1988 and 1992, President Bush defined educational reforms in partisan ideological terms, supporting schools of choice

**TABLE 5.1    Federal Educational Policy Terms**

| Pre-1980 Terms | Post-1980 Terms |
| --- | --- |
| Equity | Excellence; Standards of Performance |
| Needs and Access | Ability; Selectivity; Minimum Standards |
| Social and Welfare Concerns | Economic and Productivity Concerns |
| Common School | Parental Choice; Institutional Competition |
| Regulations, Enforcement | Deregulation |
| Federal Interventions | State and Local Initiatives |
| Diffusion of Innovations | Exhortation; Information Sharing |

Source: Clark, David and Terry Astuto, "The Disjunction of Federal Educational Policy and National Educational Needs in the 1990s." In *Education Politics for the New Century*, edited by Douglas E. Mitchell and Margaret E. Goertz, p. 13. Copyright 1990 by Taylor & Francis. Reprinted by permission.

and vouchers as expressions of the Republican Party's belief in market-based competition and enhanced consumer choice.

The 1992 Clinton-Bush presidential race demonstrated how educational policy has become more politicized. In the late 1980s, the Republican Party initiated a national debate over the importance of family values and the failings of public institutions, including schools. Candidate Bill Clinton and many other state and local Democratic candidates entered the values debate without supporting Republican approaches to change. Many democratic governors emphasized improvements in the existing public education system as opposed to proposals to privatize public schools. The 1992 and 1994 elections both resulted in the largest turnover of Congressional members since 1949. President Clinton's Democratic Administration and Secretary of Education William Riley introduced school reforms to federal politics from their years of experience as leading governors in the education reform movement. Differences between President Clinton and Republican leaders center on public versus privatized approaches to school reform.

Political observers argue that President Clinton's support for public school choice and charter schools demonstrates bipartisan support for market-like reforms. Yet the details of implementing schools of choice proposals helps distinguish political positions. The Clinton Administration has consistently opposed reforms based directly on market principles, such as unregulated competition, privatization, and public support for private schools. Conservative economists and groups within the Republican Party have long advocated school vouchers, consumer preference, and privatization as demonstrations of a free-market ideology.

Distinctions between political positions at the state and local levels of government are less clear. Political cultures and party platforms vary from state to state. Governors and legislators debate the details of school reform in relation to partisan positions, but they are also sensitive to economic conditions, popular opinion, and political expediency. Inconsistencies in partisan approaches to school reform are inevitable.

The charter school concept for changing school governance is an interesting barometer of political ideology. Many education reformers have questioned charter schools as no more than an attempt by conservative political interests to repackage or disguise school of choice and voucher proposals. However, charter schools have gained bipartisan support from state-level policy makers in ten states. In the spirit of "reinventing government" many Democrats support charter schools as an opportunity for systemic reform within the public educational system. Republicans support charter schools as an opportunity to demonstrate the positive aspects of consumer choice and school-based competition.[11]

Partisan politics is not restricted to campaign rhetoric and political platforms. As the fourth sector in educational governance, the media often attempts to highlight partisan ideological differences over politically charged educational issues such as censorship, prayer in the schools, and outcome-based education. Special interest groups are aligned with particular political ideologies and politicians with similar views. The National Education Association, for example, has consistently supported the election of Democratic presidents and members of Congress who favor increased federal support for education. The research community is not immune to political controversy. Questions have been raised, for example, about the objectivity of the research in *Politics, Markets, and America's Schools*. Joel Spring concludes: "The Republican agenda is reflected in Chubb and Moe's conclusion that the major hope for American schools is the introduction of a choice plan. From the standpoint of the politics of research, it is not surprising that their study was in part financed by the Republican-controlled U.S. Department of Education which, at the time of their research, was headed by a strong advocate of choice, Secretary of Education William Bennett."[12] However, Spring did not mention that during the period the book was written, both authors were employees of the Brookings Institute, which has long been associated with liberal political values.

Decentralization and site-based management are advocated by liberal and conservative political interests. Both political parties profess a strong belief in decentralizing the public school bureaucracy; but politicians themselves often argue for decentralization for different reasons and with opposing goals in mind. Decentralization can be proposed to enhance teacher professionalism, which is consistent with past Democratic political positions. However, decentralization can be pursued as a way to increase parental choice, reflecting the language of Republican political ideology. Compounding the confusion of political posturing in school reform is the principle of nonpartisan local school boards and special elections. As governing bodies, local school boards are ostensibly removed from partisan politics even though politics is at the heart of school reform in many communities.

## COMMUNITY POLITICS IN EDUCATION

The purpose of local control of schools is to allow communities to tailor teaching and learning to the characteristics and needs of the population. Every local school district deals with problems and policies unique to its setting and its members. The diversity of approaches to schooling in the United States is a testimony to the application of community values to the schools through the governance process.

However, serious disagreements in community values often occur in relation to public education. Issues as controversial as censorship, religious freedom, and equal rights are more likely to be debated in school board meetings than in any other community forum. Competition and conflict in the pursuit of public values pose major problems for educators. It seems that no matter what values are reflected in the curriculum, they are bound to offend some group. Debates over multi-culturalism, for example, are the outcome of an increasingly diverse and pluralistic society that comes together in the schools. Although diversity is valued in the abstract, it remains the basis of serious conflict. Arguments over "politically correct" values and "family" values frequently emanate from participation in public education. These conflicts are inevitable, given the democratic and value laden nature of schools as *public* institutions.

## Demographic Trends

The closeness of fit between a community's political culture and its school district is an important consideration for policy makers and administrators. Community demographics provide educators critical information on changes in public and private values that play a large role in shaping the politics of school governance.

The demographic picture of an educational system is one of people in motion, people moving from preschool to elementary and secondary school and often into post-secondary education and graduate school. Educational demographers attempt to explain and predict how changes in the composition of the population moving through the schools will affect policies and programs. "Schools are profoundly affected by population forces because trends in births, immigration, and migration patterns determine the number of school children, the nature of the school population, and the characteristics of children in schools in different areas and regions of the nation.[13] Recent demographic trends show the population in American schools to be more diverse than any time in history. It is also a population that is changing and diversifying more rapidly—in language, culture, social class, and life-style.

In the postwar "baby boom" generation, more than 80 percent of children grew up in a family with two biological parents who were married to each other. By 1980 only 50 percent of American children could expect to spend their entire childhood in an intact family.[14] A growing proportion of children live in homes with only one biological parent and/or a combination of adults and children from other parents. These changes in marital and domestic relations have obscured the traditional definitions of *family*. There are fewer traditional nuclear families in the 1990s than in the decades when most school systems were established.

The implications of alternative family structures are a sensitive issue for educational planners and policy makers. James Ward cautioned: "one should not assume that such 'nontraditional' households are necessarily a source of social instability, but they are merely an indicator that family support for children in such households may be diminished."[15] However, recent studies show that divorce and family disruption negatively affect school achievement. For example, children in disrupted families are nearly twice as likely as those in intact families to drop out of high school.[16]

On average, students in American schools come from poorer families than in past generations. In 1990, the United States had the highest child poverty rate of any industrialized country. According to a report by the Children's Defense Fund, 23 percent of children under six are living in poverty, a higher percentage than any other age group and more than double the rate for adults. Five million young children live in families below the poverty line. Of this number, 2.1 million are white, 1.6 million are black, 1 million are Hispanic, and 300,000 are from other minorities such as Asian or Native American.[17] Most of the families of poor children have at least one parent working. Welfare is the exclusive source of income in 25 percent of poor households. Many poor families live in costly metropolitan areas with earnings close to the poverty line, suggesting there are hundreds of thousands of additional children living in economically marginal conditions.

The ethnic composition of the United States is changing rapidly. Data from the 1990 Census indicate that from 1980 to 1990, the total U.S. population grew 9.8 percent. The White population increased by 6 percent, while minority populations increased more rapidly. The Black population grew by 13.2 percent, Native American by 37.9 percent, Hispanic by 53 percent, and Asian or Pacific Islander grew by 107.8 percent. Minorities in 1990 constituted 25 percent of the total population and approximately 35 percent of the school-age population. The population of minorities in this country is younger than the White population and tends to have more children.[18] Demographers are reasonably certain that the White segment of the American population will continue to shrink, due to further large-scale immigration, both legal and illegal, and the differentiated birth rate between white and most nonwhite ethnic groups. Some demographers refer to the "browning" of America, and predict that by 2050, Caucasians will become a minority.[19]

The combined effects of population growth and rapid political change in third world nations are increasing the rate of immigration to America. Predictions are that as many as 15 million immigrants will arrive in the United States each decade for the next thirty years.[20] The arrival of greater numbers of immigrants from many different countries is creating highly diverse communities, particularly in large coastal states such as California, Texas, and Florida. The general characteristics of the immigrant population are different from those in the last few decades. New arrivals generally have lower levels of work-related skills than the native-born population. They are poorer and have a higher rate of participation in welfare programs than in the past. Between 1986 and 1991, the number of students in American schools with little or no knowledge of English increased by 50 percent, from 1.5 million to 2.3 million. In California public schools one out of six students was born outside the United States, and one in three speaks a language other than English at home.[21] Assimilation problems are particularly acute in financially troubled school systems which must accommodate students and families representing many different cultures and languages.

Another important demographic trend affecting education is the average age of the American population. In the 1990s and beyond, the age cohort of people over 35 will grow faster than younger cohorts. There will be many more elderly people by the early twenty-first century. In 1960, there were only 16.6 million Americans aged sixty-five and over. By 1990, that figure had doubled to approximately 31 million. This older cohort is forecast to grow to 52 million in 2020 and to 65.5 million in 2030, by which time their will be more elderly people than children. The numbers of people over seventy-five and even over eighty-five will grow faster than any other age cohort.[22] Analyses of the 1990 Federal Census confirm that families with school-aged children make up a smaller percentage of the U.S. population. In 1950, 46.3 percent of American households had children under eighteen. That percentage has consistently declined to 34.6 percent in 1990. The net result is large overall declines in the proportion of young families. The "graying" of America translates to increased political power among those who do not have children in school and a concomitant lessening of the proportion of voters with school-age children. This trend has direct implications for efforts to achieve excellence in the public schools that rely on broad public support.

## The Urban-Suburban Split

Sociological studies indicate the nature of *community* in America is changing. In 1990, nearly half of the country's population was living in suburbs, up from 25 percent in 1950 and 33 percent in 1960. During the 1980s, the urban population stabilized while rural populations actually declined in the Midwest, South and West. The population suddenly started to increase in several western states in the 1990s, with growth concentrated in suburban and metropolitan areas. Population growth has continued in the suburbs over the last four to five decades. Statistically, the United States is now a suburban nation, with rural and urban fringes or borders.[23] For an increasing number of parents, *community* refers to home life in a suburban setting and employment in a separate urban center.

As the suburbs have developed, urban problems have intensified in the last decade: gang-related violence, drug abuse, crime, congested transportation systems, air pollution, outdated infrastructure, and loss of business and industry. Cities are a declining sector in American politics as evidenced by a loss in Congressional representation and the sudden dominance of the suburban voting block in state and national elections. The shift in political power to the suburbs has prompted studies of the political culture and value systems in suburban America. Schneider concludes:

> *Suburbanization means the privatization of American life and culture.*
> *Suburban voters buy "private" government—good schools and safe*
> *streets for the people who live there. They control their local govern-*
> *ment, including taxes, spending, schools, and police. . . . As property*
> *owners, they are highly resistant to taxes, cynical about government,*
> *and resent tax dollars to be used to solve other people's problems, espe-*
> *cially when they don't believe that government can actually solve*
> *those problems. . . . They are anti-political and more interested in pri-*
> *vate security than public services.*[24]

School finance studies show that the affluent in American society have created an imbalance in school funding. Suburbanization has resulted in tight control of the political process by the economically advantaged who have maintained unequal school finance formulas. Non-elites in urban areas have a difficult time becoming politically organized and powerful enough to change school funding patterns.[25]

The growing differences between political, economic, and social conditions in suburbs and urban areas is the subject of concern for educational policy makers and reformers. Many question the ability of school systems to provide equal educational opportunities when large fiscal disparities between urban and suburban schools are present. Jonothon Kozol's book, *Savage Inequalities,* dramatizes the effects of an urban-suburban split. Children in urban schools often come from communities that are poorer, with a higher percentage of non-English speaking immigrants and minority families. Educational needs are greater in urban areas while political power is weak. Political and economic power remains in the hands of suburbanites, who are white and better educated, with schools that are already operating more effectively. Kozol explains how school finance formulas based on local property taxes institutionalize the inequities between urban and suburban school districts. "The most important difference in the urban systems, I believe, is that they are often just adjacent to the nation's richest districts, and this ever-present contrast adds a heightened bitterness to the experience of children."[26] Reflecting the politics of the urban-suburban split, Kozol concludes: "Both (urban and suburban schools) are needed for our nation's governance. But children in one set of schools are educated to be governors; children in the other set of schools are trained for being governed."[27]

Eliminating the inequities created by the urban-suburban split will require the involvement of state policy-makers in the redesign of state and district school finance systems. Differences in educational opportunity for students in urban and suburban schools also pose an ethical challenge for administrators in both the impoverished and affluent communities.

## School Board Politics

Issues related to community demographics and support for public schools are central to the role and mission of local school boards. School boards are the embodiment of representative democracy, designed to be the expression of a community's political values applied to education. Studies of local school boards describe an institution that is still an important demonstration of decentralized government and local control.[28] In many instances, local boards have become more representative of the diversity of interests in their communities. However, national surveys indicate a growing need for school board reform.

The discretion of school boards and superintendents has been diminished by increasing state control and federal mandates. School boards in many communities are becoming less relevant in school reform and have lost the public's confidence. The voting public seems indifferent to school boards as democratic institutions as evidenced by low turnouts in school board elections. Only 5 to 15 percent of eligible voters participate in many district elections. As political forums, board meetings are often mired in technical details and/or political rhetoric rather than on taking action on important policy issues. School boards are criticized as elitist when a majority of members come from the business community and represent the interests of the private sector over the concerns of minority groups, educators, and the economically disadvantaged. Roughly 93 percent of local board members in the United States are White. Only 3 percent are African American and the remaining 2 percent are Hispanic, American Indian, and Asian. Sixty-four percent are men and 76 percent are over the age of forty.[29] Characterizations of community power structures demonstrate the ways in which local elites act behind the scenes to control decision making through an alignment of values and subsequent agreements between school boards and appointed superintendents.

Despite these problems, surveys show the public prefers the institution of local school boards over political authority at higher levels of government. Due to the increasing role of state government in public education, supporters of local school boards have encouraged the states to assume greater responsibility for enabling school boards to become more important policy boards: "Reforms must occur because this eighteenth century institution, reformed only once in the early twentieth century, is not structurally suited to govern effectively in an increasingly divisive society that is facing unprecedented economic and social challenges."[30] Some of the more popular school board reforms are described in Chapter 6.

## School Building and Classroom Politics

If the politics of education is directed at community concerns as opposed to national reforms, governance issues surface in the classroom as well as in district offices and school board meetings. Describing the school as the center of change shifts school improvement efforts from traditional top-down policy approaches to reforms generated and carried out by educators in schools. Research consistently demonstrates the high degree of influence teachers have over state policy mandates. In the implementation of California's mathematics curriculum, for example, some teachers simply avoided or ignored new policies, while others reinterpreted policies to match their school culture and teaching style.[31]

Recognizing the importance of school sites in governance requires a change in emphasis of the politics of education to the classroom and building levels. Micropolitics is the use of formal and informal power by individuals and groups to achieve their goals within organizations.[32] Micropolitics includes the study of both conscious and unconscious efforts to influence, persuade, guide, and control the actions of others in schools. A micropolitical view dramatically broadens the dimensions of governance in schools. Ways in which teachers, students, parents, and other groups participate in the exchange of interpersonal power are part of the overall governance process.

Micropolitical and interpersonal dimensions of governance have received far less attention than the macropolitics of state and federal educational policy. The increased involvement of governors and presidents in school reform creates a sense that the policy process is far from a local concern. However, classroom-level politics directly impact students and their developing sense of authority and organizational control. Educational governance needs to be evaluated from a personal perspective in schools as well as from the perspective of school board performance or district policies. Micropolitics emphasizes that governance originally derives from individual interactions between educators and children in schools. Consequently, the importance of personal values and political conditions in and around schools cannot be overstated. Sarason has written extensively about the influence of governance at the school and classroom level:

> *No working person (and no child in school) is unaware that his or her personal outlook, stability, and self-esteem are very much affected by how he or she is governed.*
> *The "governors" of educational policy may adopt, proclaim, and take steps to implement a policy, but if that policy is not explicitly and directly geared to alter what goes on in the classroom—especially in regard to alteration in power relationships—the policy is an exercise either in futility or irrelevance, or both.*[33]

Studies of political factors in education begin to reveal many opportunities and issues facing school administrators. As political environments, schools are both the transmitters of public values and the centers of community politics. Educational governance begins to take on broad and important dimensions for the entire school community.

## CULTURAL VALUES

Categorizing all the factors that influence the politics of education does not address their interrelationships and deeper meanings. Although it is essential to recognize the variety of external and internal variables affecting schools, it is more important to determine how they interact to shape the policy-making environment. As the political scientist David Easton argues: "In and of themselves facts do not enable us to explain or understand an event. Facts must be ordered in some way so that we can see their connection."[34] Explanatory models are needed to lend some degree of predictability to public organizations. School systems are particularly challenging to understand and decode. Those people involved in or affected by the environment of public education need more than facts and data to make effective governance decisions.

Cultural constructs are increasingly being used to understand and manage work groups and subdivisions within organizations. Culture is reflected in the codes, rituals, and distinctive patterns of behavior that guide social action. Culture shapes institutions and traditions, including how educational resources are used, what goals are pursued, and what the political environment in schools is like.[35]

## States as Political Subcultures

Subcultures of political values are spread throughout a decentralized system of educational governance. Each of the fifty states represents a political subculture, with its own priorities, state policies, and cultural traditions. Religious, social, and ethnic values evolve in ways that contribute to a state's political culture and shape its distribution of political power. Studies of everything from voting patterns to consumer habits are constantly being conducted for political campaigns, private businesses, and public agencies interested in the latest cultural trends. State education agencies attempt to assess political and social conditions to gauge the feasibility of bond elections, and tax-related legislation.

Political culture refers to the attitudes, beliefs, and sentiments which give order and meaning to a political process. Elazar's studies of state politics describe three related factors that determine the orientation and impact of political culture:

1. The set of perceptions of what politics is and what can be expected from government.
2. The kinds of people who become active in government and politics.
3. The actual way in which the art of government is practiced by citizens, politicians, and public officials.[36]

Each state's political culture is expressed through the iterative process of policy making, in which priorities are directly or indirectly identified among cultural values. Studies of state policy making, based on profiles of social, political and economic characteristics, present different pictures of the hierarchy of political authority in education. Each state is a collection of political subcultures, composed of many more subcultures and special interest groups. Within one state, groups may be seeking more equitable allocation of educational resources, while others are more interested in educational excellence within the allocation. A recent study of state educational policies depicts considerable differences in state political cultures.[37] Some states are efficiency oriented in their allocation of school finance dollars to offset some of the costs of local districts. Other states are less involved in local district operations and more invested in retaining local control as an expression of the value of liberty.

Many of the states' political culture can be expected to change as a result of demographic trends described earlier in this chapter. California, Florida, and Texas, for example, are experiencing a rapid increase in the Hispanic proportion of the population and a lowering of the average age of residents. Despite the costs and time involved in tracking changes of this magnitude, obtaining information about a states' political climate has become an important component of policy making.

## The Culture of Schools and Classrooms

The quality and character of a school culture is widely recognized as a fundamental element in creating a supportive learning environment. Individual schools and classrooms have been the subject of numerous studies using cultural constructs. Schools are not only formal organizations but also small societies where the nature of social relations significantly influences the overall operations of the society of the school.[38]

There are many approaches to the study of the subculture of schools that date back to the turn of the century. Early empirical studies were described in terms of the psychological implications of school *climate*. Recent classroom research includes teacher commitment, academic expectations, constancy of goals, and teachers' use of rewards and praise. Some studies examine *ecological* characteristics such as school size and physical space, while others discuss the classroom *milieu*, based on descriptors of teacher and student morale. Still others look at variables from the perspective of organizational theory, including bureaucratic norms and administrative control. More recently, educational anthropologists have looked at the activities, traditions, and rituals of teachers and administrators in relationship to political belief systems. The importance of shared values in schools has received considerable attention, including norms for instruction that relate to beliefs about students' abilities to learn, about classroom conduct, and the futures to which students are being directed.

Learning cultures are built on beliefs about knowledge, teaching, and personal growth. The rich and eclectic history of education and human development emphasizes caring, creativity, experimentation, and individual commitment as fundamental values. Learning environments require conditions and spaces in which knowledge can be explored and tested. New kinds of skills are practiced and critiqued. In order for learning to occur, individuals and groups need to try out different ways of thinking, conversing, and collaborating without some of the pressures of the external world. The language of learning is intersubjective, person-to-person, and having to do with people reaching understanding.[39]

Dewey emphasized that the social interactions of schooling are a critical component of a democratic learning culture.[40] He stressed that social relations in schools are not simply a mechanism for accomplishing some other aim but rather *are* education itself. The learning environment is a distinctive workplace where social relations among adults and students comprise a sense of community. School activities are opportunities for informal, sincere interactions. Social bonding among individuals is nurtured within a culture and an ethic of caring. Recent reports and analyses of effective schools stress the importance of positive learning environments, collaboration, and a widely shared sense of community.[41]

Understanding schools as learning cultures shifts the focus of reform. Educators seeking more parental involvement and public support argue that greater levels of trust from the community will lead to more constructive learning cultures. Schools would be re-organized to better support internal staff relationships in order to eliminate problems of isolated teachers and administrators. Demands for measurable outcomes and efficiency gains would be balanced with other important social and developmental goals.

## Professional Cultures

Professions can be examined as cultures with particular values, norms, rituals, internalized rules, and ways of determining membership.[42] In public education, teachers and administrators generally define themselves as *professionals*. Studies of the teaching profession and school reforms based on the professional teaching model emphasize the values and norms associated with learning cultures. Among other things, a professional teacher is expected to be dedicated to personal growth, caring, and human development.

Studies of the characteristics of educational administrators as professionals focus on their selection, preparation, and representation of community values. The demographic characteristics of school administrators are marked by an underrepresentation of women in leadership positions. Women comprise a majority of the nation's public school teaching force, representing 70 percent of all elementary, middle school, and secondary teachers. However, in the 1991–92 school year, only 5.6 percent of superintendents were women, even though administrators are drawn from the ranks of teachers. Women have consistently made up only half of the enrollments in educational administration preparation programs since the mid-1980s.[43] A similar demographic pattern is evident among state-level policy makers and administrators. Studies of the conditions leading to female underrepresentation have identified numerous structural and cultural barriers. Advocates of greater gender and racial diversity in education fault policies in the 1980s that de-emphasized equity and gender concerns in favor of reforms directed at educational excellence and international competitiveness.

Educational administration is organized around many of the same principles that are applied to managing private sector organizations. The administrative profession defines schools in bureaucratic terms; educational-environments need managing, with clear rules and rational procedures designed for order and efficiency. These technical, science-based principles have been described as "cognitive-instrumental," in which all aspects of administration are rationalized.[44] A distinct language has emerged from the rational-instrumental view of organizations that stresses the values of efficiency and expediency:

> *It is a language of administration and law, an instrumental language of getting things done. It speaks of goals and objectives, maximization, implementation, standardization, validity, accountability, planning, rules, regulations, measurement, and consistency. The language suggests a particular way of thinking, a particular view of the world. . . . It is a language derived from the sciences, law, and economics.*[45]

The administrative culture is fundamentally about getting things done. School reforms based on total quality management (TQM) testify to the continued emphasis on business and industrial management procedures, the objectification of knowledge, and market-oriented metaphors for schools and social relations.

The culture and language of administration is different from and often at odds with the values, assumptions, and conditions within a learning culture. A clash of professional cultures between teachers and administrators often occurs, causing conflict, confusion, and disharmony. Differences in professional cultures are most evident within the realm of assessing and measuring performance in schools. Administrative reforms often rely on quantitative data collection and the application of statistical procedures to standardize outcomes.[46] TQM does not value other data sources and methods such as interviews, observations, critical ethnography, and narrative storytelling that emanate from other perspectives within a learning culture. A managerial emphasis on impersonal and standardized outcomes exacerbates tensions with teachers who focus more on personal classroom experiences and practices. Foster[47] argues that when educational communities are subjected to standards of efficiency, accountability, and predictability as applied to other technical and scientific enterprises, they are bureaucratized by demands that do not support other democratic roles and responsibilities.

School reformers frequently advocate for the values and approaches of one professional culture over another. For purposes of understanding the nature of the governance environment, it's important to recognize the presence of different belief systems and the probability of conflict and misunderstandings between both teachers and administrators as professional groups.

# ASSESSING AND MANAGING CULTURES

The last decade has witnessed a plethora of training programs, commercial publications, and academic texts that prescribe ways of understanding and managing organizational cultures.[48] Challenges brought on by social, racial, and ethnic diversity in many communities have led to cultural approaches to school administration. Educators are urged to create a common vision and a positive culture for learning. Scholars suggest that the social and moral values of common schooling in the history of education have been reinterpreted in the 1990s through reforms designed to manage school cultures and create a positive sense of community.[49]

One of the more profound and contentious policy debates in the 1900s concerns the socioeconomic background of students and the impact of culture on school performance. Brought about in part by the urban and suburban split described earlier, policy makers are divided over the problem of inequities between school districts. Questions are surfacing about whether additional financial resources for urban schools are as effective as changing the cultural mix of students within urban settings. James Traub argues:

> It is values and culture, not resources, that determine academic outcomes; and middle-class children bring with them to school values that produce success—self discipline, a faith in institutions and their rules, and above all, an expectation of success itself. Poor kids, by contrast, often reach school with the cognitive problems that come from having poorly educated or disengaged or preoccupied parents as well as with the assumptions appropriate to their experience.[50]

Even though schools are important social and intellectual forces, they are far less influential than a child's home environment. Reforms that emanate from this view would intermix students from different sociocultural backgrounds. These policies usually mean moving poor students and families from impoverished city neighborhoods to wealthier suburban neighborhoods or movement in the reverse direction. This approach has been repeatedly rejected in suburban neighborhoods, as have attempts to move tax dollars from wealthy suburban areas to poorer urban school districts.

School reforms that formally recognize and attempt to manipulate cultural factors trigger several practical and ethical questions. When culture is viewed as the means of reform, educators are urged to manage cultural elements. These forces are complex and easily oversimplified. If culture is viewed as the object of reform, change efforts could be naive and unduly optimistic. Cultural values are both enduring and elusive, and less subject to direct manipulation than advocates would like to believe.[51] There are moral and philosophical issues involved in using social and cultural elements as instruments of management and control. The distinction between private and public life becomes blurred when factors related to family origin are used to change the composition and quality of public institutions.

A school *community* is not a fixed element that can be managed and manipulated. Educators must deal with the dynamics of non-English speaking populations and issues of cultural literacy, which include appreciating and including nontraditional, non-Western approaches to policy making and public participation. Even though collegiality and a shared sense of community is a widely accepted principle in theory, it is difficult to support in the highly fragmented and specialized context of public education.

Practical application of cultural and political studies, from the classroom to the national level, presents a challenge for educational policy makers. There is an impressive variety of research that helps demystify the educational environment. Yet political values and cultural forces identified in this chapter are neither static or obvious at the interpersonal level. Political values are frequently submerged, subtle, and guarded in the governance process.

## POLITICAL AND CULTURAL UNCERTAINTY

Educators throughout the American system are directly affected by debates over political and cultural values. The quality and tone of the debate itself has important cultural implications for administrators and teachers. When political discourse is based on shrill rhetoric and positions stated in the extreme, compromise becomes hard to achieve. The exaggerated expression of reform values between proponents of centralization and decentralization, for example, has added bitterness to the often unproductive arguments in public education. Neither side seems to appreciate that no particular balance will remain appropriate forever.[52] Governance debates are often divisive and inconclusive when they are framed as either-or positions on the many complex value questions in education.

Educators already face high levels of uncertainty, particularly in diverse urban school districts. Organizational uncertainty is a condition in which important events cannot be predicted with any reasonable degree of probability and are assumed to be random. Such a condition has developed in many of today's public schools where traditional patterns of governance and administration are being markedly changed through state legislation, court rulings, federal mandates, and uneven district policies. Schools are inherently uncertain organizations in that the social environment is complex, unpredictable, and rapidly changing. However, schools as organizations have not developed flexible structures to deal with constant change. The net effect of ongoing political controversy transposed on an already complex and uncertain social environment is that no one can fully understand or control what is happening.

Observers of school reforms have portrayed redundant and ineffective cycles and pendulum swings in policy. Although educators are trained to welcome and encourage intellectual diversity, the cumulative effects of constant reform can create a destabilizing effect in an already uncertain environment. As an alternative, differences in values can be balanced in the form of practical policies designed to achieve equality and efficiency, community and economic growth. Educators can then proceed with a sense of support and direction. The American educational system has survived several periods of political and cultural conflict in its 200-year history. Time will tell whether the current debates over public and private values will strengthen or replace public education.

## SUMMARY

There are a multitude of factors affecting the environment of educational governance. Many come from outside the control of formal organizations and institutions. A comprehensive review of governance factors includes an analysis of political values and cultural forces, even though they are controversial and inherently difficult to measure.

Five values or objects of policy have been prominent in shaping the American educational system, each of which is rooted in political ideologies and philosophies of government. Governance is an exercise in finding a balance between competing values and political positions. Liberty, equality, efficiency, community, and economic productivity are at the core of many governance debates.

The closeness of fit between a community's political culture and its school district is an important consideration for policy makers and administrators. Community demographics provide educators critical information on changes in public and private values that play a large role in shaping the politics of school governance. Recent demographic trends suggest the population in American schools is highly diverse and changing rapidly—in language, culture, social class, and life-style. The growing differences between political, economic, and social conditions in suburbs and urban areas is the subject of concern for educational policy makers and reformers.

Educational governance can be viewed from a cultural perspective. The quality and character of a school's culture is a fundamental element in how it functions. The political culture within states, communities, and neighborhoods provides important indicators of the dynamics of educational decision making. Subcultures of political values are spread throughout a decentralized system of educational governance. Each of the fifty states represents a political subculture, with its own priorities, state policies, and cultural traditions. Many of the states' political culture can be expected to change as a result of demographic trends.

Learning cultures are built on beliefs about knowledge, teaching, and personal growth. Teachers and administrators are members of professional cultures, with particular values, norms, rituals, internalized rules, and ways of determining membership in the culture. The culture and language of administration is different from and often at odds with the values, assumptions, and conditions within a learning culture.

The social and moral values of common schooling have been reinterpreted in the 1990s through reforms designed to manage school cultures. However, school reforms that formally recognize and attempt to manipulate cultural factors trigger several practical and ethical questions. When culture is viewed as the means of reform, educators are urged to develop vision statements and manage cultural elements. These forces are complex and easily oversimplified. If culture is viewed as the object of reform, change efforts could be naive and unduly optimistic. The cumulative effects of political instability throughout the system need to be considered. School leaders need a variety of skills and sources of information to continuously assess the implications of political and cultural forces.

## SEMINAR QUESTIONS

1. How do the following factors affect the governance environment in your educational setting?

   - Community and school demographics
   - Social and political values
   - Cultural factors
   - Educational goals and purposes

2. What are the effects of partisan politics on education in your community? In your state?

3. How can the inequities between urban and suburban schools be rectified?

4. What do you think are the effects of political uncertainty on educators?

## SUGGESTED READINGS

Blase, Joseph, ed. *The Politics of Life in the Schools.* Newbury Park, California: Sage Publications, 1991.

Brown, Rexford. *Schools of Thought.* San Francisco: Jossey-Bass, 1991.

Mitchell, Douglas E. and Margaret E. Goertz, eds. *Education Politics for the New Century.* New York: Falmer Press, 1990.

Schlesinger, Arthur M., Jr. *Cycles of American History.* Boston: Houghton Mifflin, 1986.

Spring, Joel. *Conflict of Interests: The Politics of American Education.* 2nd ed. New York: Longman, 1993.

## ENDNOTES

1. David Tyack, "Ways of Seeing: An Essay on the History of Compulsory Schooling," in *History, Education, and Public Policy,* ed. Donald R. Warren (Berkeley, Calif.: McCutchan Publishing Corporation, 1978), pp. 56–89.

2. Joseph Blase, "The Micropolitical Perspective," in *The Politics of Life in the Schools* (Newbury Park, California: Sage Publications, 1991), p. 1.

3. Douglas E. Mitchell, "Education Politics for the New Century: Past Issues and Future Directions," in *Education Politics for the New Century,* eds. Douglas E. Mitchell and Margaret E. Goertz (New York: Falmer Press, 1990), pp. 153–167.

4. David P. Ericson, "On Critical Theory and Educational Practice," in *Critical Perspectives on the Organization and Improvement of Schooling,* eds. Kenneth A. Sirotnik and Jeannie Oakes (Boston: Kluver-Nijhoff Publishing, 1986), p. 209.

5. Austin D. Swanson and Richard A. King, *School Finance: Its Economics and Politics* (New York: Longman, 1991), pp. 3–4. Marshall, et al., *Culture and Education Policy,* pp. 89–92.

6. Maxine Greene, "Identities and Contours: An Approach to Educational History," in *History, Education, and Public Policy,* ed. Donald R. Warren (Berkeley, Calif.: McCutchan Publishing Corporation, 1978), pp. 296–308.

7. Arthur M. Schlesinger Jr., "The Turn of the Cycle," *The New Yorker,* (November 1992), p. 53. Also see Arthur M. Schlesinger Jr., *Cycles of American History* (Boston: Houghton Mifflin, 1986).

8. David L. Clark and Terry A. Astuto, "The Disjunction of Federal Educational Policy and National Educational Needs in the 1990s," in *Education Politics for the New Century.* eds. Douglas E. Mitchell and Margaret E. Goertz (New York: Falmer Press, 1990), pp. 11–25.

9. Ibid.
10. William L. Boyd, "The Power of Paradigms: Reconceptualizing Educational Policy and Management," *Educational Administration Quarterly,* vol. XXVIII, no. 4 (November 1992).
11. Paul Bauman, Debra Banks, Michael Murphy, and Hal Kuczwara, "The Charter School Movement: Preliminary Findings from the First Three States," unpublished paper presented at the American Educational Research Association Annual Conference, (New Orleans: April 1994), pp. 1–31.
12. Joel Spring, "Knowledge and Power in Research into Politics of Urban Education," in *The Politics of Urban Education in the United States,* eds. James G. Cibulka, Rodney J. Reed, and Kenneth K. Wong (Washington, DC: Falmer Press 1991), p. 49.
13. James G. Ward, "Analysis of Demographic Change, Cultural Diversity, and School Finance Policy," in *The New Politics of Race and Gender,* ed. Catherine Marshall (Washington, DC: Falmer Press, 1993), p. 7.
14. Barbara Dafoe Whitehead, "Dan Quayle was Right," *The Atlantic,* vol. 271, no. 4 (April 1993).
15. Ward, "Analysis of Demographic Change, Cultural Diversity, and School Finance Policy," p. 9.
16. Whitehead, "Dan Quayle was Right," *The Atlantic* (April, 1993). Whitehead cites a survey by the National Center for Health Statistics, (1988) and *Second Chances: Men, Women, and Children a Decade after Divorce* by Judith Wallerstein and Sandra Blakeslee (1989).
17. Jacqueline P. Danzberger, Michael W. Kirst, and Michael D. Usdan, *Governing Public Schools: New Times New Requirements* (Washington, DC: Institute for Educational Leadership, 1992), pp. 2–3.
18. Ward, "Analysis of Demographic Change, Cultural Diversity, and School Finance Policy," p. 22.
19. William A. Henry, "Beyond the Melting Pot," *Time,* (April 9, 1990), pp. 28–35.
20. Paul Kennedy, *Preparing for the Twenty-First Century* (New York: Random House, 1993), p. 313.
21. Paul Grey, "Teach Your Children Well," *Time* (Fall 1993), pp. 69–75. Grey cites 1993 studies of the impacts of immigration policies by the Urban Institute and the Rand Corporation. Also see "American Survey: Return of the Huddled Masses," *The Economist* (May 7, 1994), pp. 25–26.
22. Kennedy, *Preparing for the Twenty-First Century,* p. 311.
23. William Schneider, "The Suburban Century Begins," *The Atlantic Monthly* (July 1992), pp. 37–38. Also see Karl Jackson, *Crabgrass Frontier: The Suburbanization of the United States* New York: Oxford University Press, 1985).
24. Schneider, "The Suburban Century Begins," p. 37.
25. Ward, "Analysis of Demographic Change, Cultural Diversity, and School Finance Policy," p. 12.
26. Jonothon Kozol, *Savage Inequalities* (New York: Crown Publishers, 1991), pp. 74–75.
27. Ibid, p. 75.
28. Jacqueline P. Danzberger, Michael W. Kirst, and Michael D. Usdan, *Governing Public Schools: New Times New Requirements* (Washington, DC: Institute for

Educational Leadership, 1992), p. xii. Also see Michael W. Kirst, "Who Would Control the Schools? Reassessing Current Policies," in *Schooling for Tomorrow: Directing Reforms to Issues That Count,* ed. Thomas J. Sergiovanni and John H. Moore (Boston: Allyn & Bacon, 1989), pp. 62–87.

29. Steven Porter, *Wisdoms Passing* (New York: Barclay House, 1989), p. 36.
30. Jacqueline P. Danzberger, "Governing the Nation's Schools: The Case for Restructuring Local School Boards," *Phi Delta Kappan* (January 1994), p. 371.
31. David K. Cohen and Deborah L. Ball, "Relations between Policy and Practice: A Commentary," *Educational Evaluation and Policy Analysis,* vol. 12, no. 3 (Fall 1990), pp. 249–256. Linda Darling-Hammond, "Instructional Policy into Practice: 'The Power of the Bottom over the Top,'" *Educational Evaluation and Policy Analysis,* vol. 12, no. 3 (Fall 1990), pp. 233–241.
32. Joseph Blase, "The Micropolitical Perspective," in *The Politics of Life in the Schools,* ed. Joseph Blase (Newbury Park, California: Sage Publications, 1991), pp. 1–18.
33. Seymour B. Sarason, *The Case for Change: Rethinking the Preparation of Educators* (San Francisco: Jossey-Bass, 1993), p. 166.
34. David Easton, *The Political System* (New York: Alfred A. Knopf, 1953), p. 4.
35. Catherine Marshall, et al., *Culture and Education Policy in the American States* (New York: Falmer Press, 1989).
36. Daniel J. Elazar, *American Federalism,* 3rd ed. (New York: Harper and Row, 1984), p. 112.
37. Marshall, et al., *Culture and Education Policy.*
38. Anthony S. Byrk, Valerie E. Lee, and Julia B. Smith, "High School Organization and Its Effects on Teachers and Students: An Interpretive Summary of the Research," in *Choice and Control in American Education,* vol. 1, ed. William H. Clune and John F. Witte (New York: Falmer, 1990). Byrk cites William Waller, *The Sociology of Teaching* (New York: Russell & Russell, 1932).
39. Rexford Brown, *Schools of Thought* (San Francisco: Jossey-Bass, 1991), p. 162.
40. John Dewey, *Democracy and Education* (New York: Macmillan, 1916), pp. 7–8.
41. Roland Barth, *Improving Schools from Within* (San Francisco: Jossey-Bass, 1990). Rexford Brown, *Schools of Thought* (San Francisco: Jossey-Bass, 1991). Thomas J. Sergiovanni, *Moral Leadership: Getting to the Heart of School Improvement* (San Francisco: Jossey-Bass, 1992). Susan J. Rosenholtz, *Teacher's Workplace: The Social Organization of Schools* (White Plains, NY: Longman, 1989).
42. Donald A. Schon, *Educating the Reflective Practitioner* (San Francisco: Jossey-Bass, 1990).
43. Colleen Bell and Susan Chase "The Underrepresentation of Women in School Leadership," in *The New Politics of Race and Gender,* ed. Catherine Marshall (Washington, DC: Falmer Press, 1993), pp. 141–154.
44. William Foster, "A Critical Perspective on Administration and Organization in Education," pp. 95–129, in *Critical Perspectives on the Organization and Improvement of Schooling,* eds. Kenneth A. Sirotnik and Jeannie Oakes (Boston: Kluver-Nijhoff Publishing, 1986).
45. Brown, *Schools of Thought,* p. 157.

46. Colleen A. Capper and Michael T. Jamison, "Let the Buyer Beware: Total Quality Management and Education Research and Practice," *Educational Researcher,* vol. 22, no. 8 (November 1993), pp. 26–27.

47. Foster, "A Critical Perspective on Administration and Organization in Education," p. 121.

48. For a history of the use of cultural constructs in organizational management, see J. Steven Ott, *The Organizational Culture Perspective* (Pacific Grove, Calif. Brooks/Cole Publishing, 1989). Also see Ann Lieberman, *Schools as Collaborative Cultures: Creating the Future Now* (New York: Falmer Press, 1990).

49. Thomas J. Sergiovanni, et al., *Educational Governance and Administration* (Boston: Allyn & Bacon, 1992). For a critique of recent efforts to manage or change communities in relation to schools and other public agencies, see Thomas Bender, *Community and Social Change in America* (New Brunswick: Rutgers University Press, 1978).

50. James Traub, "Can Separate Be Equal? New Answers to an Old Question about Race and Schools," *Harper's* (June 1994), p. 44.

51. Douglas E. Mitchell, "Education Politics for the New Century: Past Issues and Future Directions," in *Education Politics for the New Century,* eds. Douglas E. Mitchell and Margaret E. Goertz (New York: Falmer Press, 1990), pp. 153–167.

52. Michael B. Katz, *Reconstructing American Education* (Cambridge, Mass.: Harvard University Press, 1987), p. 119.

# 6

## REFORMING SCHOOL AND
## SYSTEM-WIDE GOVERNANCE

*The locomotive of history cannot be switched onto a
new track all that easily. But revolutionary strategy
may provide at least the possibility of a new roadbed.*
—James MacGregor Burns

School reforms have been attempted since the beginning of the
American educational system. Historians and scholars have portrayed
movements, trends, waves, and cycles of reform along with detailed
accounts of their successes and failures. The undercurrents of school
reform in the 1990s are fundamentally different from the spirit of past
school improvement efforts. Policy makers and parents are engaged in
intense debates about the survival of public education itself. There are
serious questions about the utility of common schooling in a diverse and
technologically advanced society. National, state, and local initiatives
directed at teaching and learning are continuing; but they are increasingly overshadowed by reforms designed to fundamentally change the
organization and political control of public education.

Proposed changes in governance range from improvements in
school boards to the replacement of public governance with privatized
schools of choice. Many of the system-wide governance reforms in education reflect popular political views directed at other components of
government. The broad philosophical underpinnings of these proposals
and the diversity of reforms already underway in education requires an
examination of many different approaches to change. This chapter will

review reforms that are directed specifically at school governance as well as other proposals that indirectly affect school and system-wide decision making.

## THE CONTEXT OF SCHOOL REFORM

In order to examine the impacts of system-wide school reforms on the process of governance, the conditions created by ten years of nationwide efforts at educational change need to be considered. Scholars have characterized and classified two recent waves of reform. The first wave is associated with the eight- to ten-year period following the publication of *A Nation At Risk,* the often cited report by the National Commission on Excellence in Education in 1983.[1] Studied and evaluated in considerable detail, the first wave is described as a policy-driven, top-down era of reform in which governors, state legislators, and national commissions became heavily involved in efforts to improve standards and the overall performance of students.[2] Issues such as teacher competence, the utility and validity of standardized testing, and other pedagogical questions received considerable attention. Research findings on the status of every aspect of public schooling were published by public and private organizations. Reports that inventory and evaluate all types of reforms are available.[3]

The energy and creativity behind this first wave of reform was unprecedented. Over 300 commissions and committees were formed across the states in the early 1980s to raise standards and strengthen graduation requirements.[4] Governors and state-level business groups were particularly active in proposing system-wide policy changes. This first wave attracted new actors into the complex enterprise of public education with new views of organizational change and different approaches to thinking about reform.

The desire for more fundamental change increased. As the decade progressed many educators, researchers, and parents became concerned that many reforms were either misdirected, not working, or insufficient. Michael Cohen wrote "the demands on the educational system . . . far outstrip its capacity to respond and will continue to do so as long as schools remain in their current form."[5] It became clear that the involvement of powerful forces from outside the school systems was raising expectations for bigger and bolder changes. Rather than what was perceived as tinkering with the current system, some educators and business groups began calling for a major overhaul of the entire enterprise.

Debates shifted from teaching and learning to the nature of reform itself. Those familiar with past reform movements challenged the assumption that change should be driven from outside the system by the increasing number of coalitions and critical groups.[6] Many emphasized that school sites should be the focus and impetus of reform, while others stressed the importance of national standards and changes in state policies. Representatives from within the educational community and from external organizations began to question whether school reforms really could make any difference, given the size of the American system, with its increasing diversity and complexity. Glickman's observation in 1990 captured a growing sense that "the results of restructuring efforts have been more rhetorical than real."[7]

These views broadened the school reform movement without diminishing the level of interest from the first wave. The term *systemic change* entered the lexicon of school improvement and debates intensified around institutional barriers to reform. In essence, it became clear to policy makers, researchers, and parents that it was time to look beyond particular aspects of teaching, learning, and testing and consider the effectiveness of the entire system.

The second wave of reform directed attention to structural and organizational dimensions of public education. The emphasis on high standards and expectations for student learning, as well as improvements in the quality of teaching continued. However, the second wave added organizational and managerial dimensions of public schooling. The language of reform began to incorporate concepts and theories associated with political action and organizational change from the private sector. The calls for reform became more intense than the rhetoric behind the first wave in the early 1980s. The second wave questioned everything about the existing system and demanded fundamental restructuring.

The new emphasis on organizational factors set the stage for greater interest in educational governance in the 1990s. Research showed that the structural components of governance were largely overlooked in the first wave of reform.[8] In the 1990s however, all aspects of governance are being questioned. The combined effects of the first and second waves has generated several system-wide and politicized reform agendas designed to bring about fundamental changes in educational decision making.

## DECENTRALIZATION

Decentralization is defined in managerial terms as a wider distribution of power and authority in and among organizations.[9] In educational settings, decentralization is the intended effect of site-based or school-based management which redistributes decision-making authority.

Proposals advocating schools of choice also emphasize the value and benefits of decentralizing bureaucratic educational settings. Top-down structures common to most school districts are replaced by collaborative relationships between groups and levels of educators and administrators within the school and the district. In structural terms, decentralization moves authority down from a hierarchical and autocratic chain of command to a flatter and more collaborative decision-making model.

There are dozens of names, acronyms, and phrases representing plans to decentralize public school governance. They include school-based management, site-based management, collaborative decision making, site-based decision making, and shared decision making. The term empowerment includes the principles of decentralizing authority and the professionalization of teachers.[10] A publication sponsored by the U.S. Department of Education defines *site-based management (SBM)* as follows: "SBM aims to *decentralize decision making* by transferring authority from state education agencies and school district offices to units such as governance councils, committees or teams located at the school."[11] The emphasis on shifting decision making in this definition underscores the degree to which governance is the focus of decentralization.

Decentralization is a primary goal and a political value within most restructuring plans. Yet the variety of approaches to organizational and behavioral change may not be identified as political reform. Decentralization can be misleading in the sense that it sounds like objective, structural change in an organization. However, it primarily involves shifts in authority and changes in the balance of power between people. Consequently, the political and interpersonal dimensions of decentralization plans must be carefully considered.

## Politics of Decentralization

The political philosophy supporting decentralization is evident in the design of the American federalist system. Authority to provide free, public education has been delegated and decentralized from the federal level to state governments, who in turn decentralize decision making further to local school districts. The proper placement of political authority is central to both the theory and the successful implementation of school decentralization plans. The principle behind site-based management is participatory democracy. Smaller governing bodies are seen as representing a wide cross-section of educators and community members at the school level who should help determine policies that directly affect them. Theoretically, greater participation in decision making helps build consensus for certain reforms and helps ensure that the changes reflect the expertise of those directly involved in teaching and learning.

Three general arguments for decentralization in educational settings have been identified.[12]

1. The *redistribution* argument emphasizes the value of power sharing between organizational units of government. Weiler's research on national and state governments demonstrates how power is shared through the allocation of resources and decision-making authority. Distribution arguments stress the benefits of making decisions at the local level. People closest to the issues are presumed to know best what the solutions are, but need greater authority to solve local problems.

2. The second argument for decentralization is based on *efficiency*. Decentralization is believed to enhance the cost-effectiveness of the educational system through a more efficient deployment and management of resources. Reinforcing the first argument, if people closest to the issues are best at identifying and solving problems, they will generate more efficient solutions.

3. The third argument stresses decentralization in order to support *cultures of learning*. Creating positive learning environments requires greater decision making authority over academic content at the school site. Curricula can be made more relevant to local concerns and community resources can be more easily incorporated into the learning environment.

These three arguments represent the philosophy of decentralization in different yet complimentary ways. They consistently stress the value of moving all aspects of decision making away from centralized government jurisdictions.

In the 1990s, decentralization is a popular political and managerial philosophy in most parts of the world. The breakup of the Soviet Union is the biggest example of political reform based on the failure of a centralized government system. In the United States, new versions of federalism are attempts to move federal programs and policy decisions to state, county, and city units of government.[13] In the private sector, businesses are emphasizing employee involvement (EI) and total quality management (TQM) to provide employees a greater role in decision making.[14] TQM programs have also been tailored to school systems and supported by public and private organizations across the country. Site-based management in education reflects many of the same principals of reform in other public organizations. Osborne and Gabler's *Reinventing Government* details a variety of decentralized approaches to public management based on case studies from cities and public agencies across the country.[15]

## *Implementation Issues and Opportunities*

Decentralization is easier to describe in theory than it is to implement in complex organizations like schools. Decentralization plans must delineate the ways in which organizational decision making is shifted in conjunction with the resources needed to carry out those decisions. Educational leaders must consider what degree of power shifts are possible, given the complex, legal dimensions of schools as public institutions. Major components of public education, from standardized tests to building designs, are either controlled or influenced by state or national government agencies or regulatory authorities. Decentralization advocates must consider the contradictions created by educational provisions in state constitutions that mandate *uniform* and *equal* educational opportunities. Administrators must consider how to change long-held patterns of political control in schools and districts. As Weiss states: "Decentralization of control can occur in many different ways, depending on which kind of control is at stake and which actors are involved. . . . General statements about the advantages or disadvantages of decentralization are far too simple to offer any guidance for policy."[16]

Effective decentralization plans require a series of interrelated conditions. First, the school site or building becomes the point of focus in efforts to improve education. The school district must then set the stage for and support decentralization efforts. In effect, the entire district decision-making structure must subscribe to changing authority patterns. Decentralization requires changes in governance and political behavior, empowering new groups and individuals who are often unaccustomed to the complexity and trade offs that important decisions present. The costs and benefits of decentralization then depend on how new individuals and groups will use information, expertise, and incentives to make good decisions.

Researchers have documented the complexity of decentralization and its inherent-contradictions.[17] Wohlstetter and Buffet found that even when school site councils were given greater authority, they rarely made substantive decisions that fully exercised their new roles.[18] "Reviews of the literature on school-site management find that the authority of schools and of school-site councils—which typically represent some combination of parents, administrators, and staff—is either very vaguely specified or highly circumscribed; seldom if ever does school-site management actually mean real control over the core elements of the organization (budgeting, staffing, curriculum, organizational structure, and governance).[19] Many believe that the potential of decentralization is far from realized, in part because the processes required to change decision-making patterns can be time-consuming, contentious, and limited in terms of eventual effects on student performance. A comprehensive study of teachers' perceptions of decentralization concluded that even in those schools that had instituted site-based management programs and had made other efforts to give teachers more autonomy, teachers perceived changes to be top-down and not designed to assist them.[20] Perhaps the most unsettling criticism is the lack of empirical evidence that decentralization plans have any effect on school efficiency and effectiveness or student performance.

Despite these concerns, decentralization plans are being implemented in school systems across the country. The empowerment of teachers and building-level administrators has been called a catalyst for major change that will promote higher teacher morale, increased community involvement in schools, and greater opportunity for educational innovation and creativity.[32] Glickman characterized the headiness of the empowerment movement as a "reaction to the heavy-handed legislative reforms of the past."[21] Research from districts that have emphasized site-based management for five years or more identified several positive consequences, including community perceptions of greater legitimacy for schools and districts, increased sensitivity to local needs on the part of school principals, and better linkages between schools and community agencies.

## CENTRALIZATION

*Centralization* per se is not being proposed by educational reformers or elected officials. The American system of decentralized state and local control is a legally organized structure established over many decades, remaining essentially unchanged since the creation of public schools. However, some school reforms have the effect of centralizing critical components of educational decision making, while others emphasize a greater federal role in state and local education programs.

Centralization is more easily recognized when it is considered in the context of *nationwide* reform. The most visible example is the movement to establish national goals and performance standards for public education. When President Bush and the fifty state governors met for an education summit in the fall of 1989, traditions of a small federal role in education were broken and a new era was inaugurated. The country now has national education goals and there is widespread talk of a national curriculum. The governors even issued a blueprint for how states can accomplish the national educational goals.[22] What traditionally accompanies national-level reforms are shifts in authority to educational policy makers responsible for defining, implementing, and evaluating nationwide objectives. Although reformers may oppose centralizing authority, they may support national reforms that require shifts in authority to higher levels of governance.

Cross-cultural comparisons of educational systems also generate support for centralized approaches to change. Publication of *A Nation At Risk* in 1982 stimulated considerable interest in European and Japanese educational systems that continues in the 1990s. Despite the considerations that must be made when comparing student populations in different countries, critics continue to point to the poor performance of students in the American system of decentralized school districts. The economist Lester Thurow states: "Consider the 15,000-plus independently elected local school boards that run America's schools—the ultimate in Jeffersonian local democracy. If an educational system that allows thousands of local school boards to run schools was a good one, one might reasonably expect that at least one of those 15,000 school systems could turn out high school graduates whose achievements could match those of Europe or Japan. None can."[23] Thurow represents the interests of many national reform advocates who believe the world's best school systems operate under a strong centralized ministry of education that sets tough standards that everyone must meet. Polls show a majority of Americans agree that national standards and nationwide efforts are needed.[24]

Authority and control can shift to higher levels of government without the organized efforts of reformers or policy makers. Centralization can occur slowly and incrementally through the authority-oriented patterns of large organizations. Centralized government agencies are typically responsible for and considered more effective and efficient at allocating resources and regulating behavior. Examples in public education include the increasing role of state governments in school finance, and the strong federal role in administering, monitoring, and evaluating categorical aide programs. State governments are capable of pursuing equitable school finance formulas in ways local governments and school districts cannot. Further, state and federal agencies can enforce regulations regarding affirmative action and equal opportunity that are beyond the scope of local school districts or units of local government.

Higher levels of government tend to consolidate authority over time. They also regain considerable control over local decision making through their centralized role in program evaluation. Studies of the first wave of school reforms in the 1980s document how this centralizing effect occurred. Efforts to raise graduation requirements and improve teaching often took the form of greater standardization and increased state regulatory activity. Though the first wave of reform produced a multitude of approaches to decentralization, the second wave includes ongoing attempts to establish a stronger role for state governments, particularly in setting goals and standards.[25]

Another view of centralization in public education is from an organizational and economic standpoint. Organizational theorists and coalitions of educational reformers depict the American system as centralized in the sense of being monopolistic, bureaucratic, and homogeneous.[26] Studies of schools and districts across the country demonstrate the similarity of school buildings, curricula, classrooms, and organizational policies. Commonalties in so many settings are viewed as demonstrations of uniformity and consistency resulting from a highly centralized governance system, despite the principles of local control and years of effort at site-based management.

## BALANCING DECENTRALIZATION AND CENTRALIZATION

The reform philosophies of decentralization and centralization seem to be working against each other, particularly when they are presented as absolute values. Centralization-decentralization arguments are often driven by political considerations and presented as if one direction or the other are all-or-nothing propositions. Educational policy-makers who support national standards and centralization face an apparent contradiction. On one hand, national coalitions of government organizations, educators and business leaders represent a high level of energy and momentum necessary to initiate major changes. On the other hand, Americans are consistently opposed to centralized authority and federal intervention in local affairs. Local control of public education is a sacred tradition in public education, even if higher levels of government are better suited to implement and oversee the democratic value of equal educational opportunity. Policy makers operating in the middle of the American system are hearing calls for greater autonomy at the local school level, while also feeling the pressure to achieve national goals and standards established by the nation's governors and U.S. presidents representing both political parties.

This apparent contradiction between centralization and decentralization is based on the assumption that both reforms can not exist simultaneously. However a balance between these two forces can be achieved, based on practical questions of where certain decisions can best be made. Madison's proposals in the *Federalist* papers written over

200 years ago recognized the need to balance political authority at different operating levels of government.[27] Some view the best model of school governance as a combination of a decentralized emphasis on teacher professionalism combined with a commitment to national standards, thereby producing a simultaneous bottoms-up–top-down approach to change.[28]

Shifts in authority between centralized and decentralized levels of government have frequently occurred in the history of public education. The American system of federal, state, and local governance has been designed and redesigned to pursue different kinds of reforms. Public education can be portrayed as centralized and monopolistic in its effects, or as a highly decentralized system based on local control. It is so large and interconnected with other social and economic institutions that generalized attempts at decentralization or centralization are often ineffective or inefficient. The value of attempting to base reform on movements between these two theoretical points of authority may be more about political turmoil outside of education than a sustained effort to determine the best way to make educational decisions.

The present system of public education is based on a series of practical compromises between national and local interests. Centralization and decentralization will continue to be represented in governance debates and reform plans. The balance between these essentially political views will require considerable efforts from the standpoint of educational governance. In order to establish a constructive approach to reform, the tendencies of large organizations to retain authority and the energies and resources of national coalitions will need to be balanced with the interests of local control and site-based decision making.

## CHOICE

Choice-driven school reforms consistently emphasize the role of parents in controlling or influencing the selection of the school site for their children. The schools of choice movement seeks to diversify education by allowing individual schools to develop programs and attract families depending on individual students' needs and interests or on family preference.[29] Although the effect of choice-based reforms could be the decentralization of public education, these approaches to school improvement are based on different views of the degree of change needed.

The concept of greater choice in education is deceptively simple in comparison with the implications of choice-based reforms. The literal meaning of the word *choice* is a highly regarded American value, associated with liberty and democratic freedom. Consequently, it is important for policy makers and parents to define the meaning and potential impacts of choice as an educational reform, as opposed to choice as a basic right and freedom to make private decisions or personal choices within public life.

## Philosophy of Choice

Choice-driven reforms assume that school decision making should be based on market forces of supply and demand, as other decisions are made in the private sector and in private life. The language employed to explain the effects of choice derives from organizational economics and capitalism. The associated theory in school reform assumes the ability to choose from an unregulated supply of schools, which will create competition and greater responsiveness on the part of school staff to the needs of clients.[30] Choice advocates are philosophically opposed to the present system of political decision making by democratically elected school boards. They believe that democratic governance makes bureaucracy inevitable and that democratic decisions are so compromised that they are confusing and contradictory.

Schools-of-choice proposals are supported by research that identifies the impacts of organizational factors on student performance. Within this area of educational research, evidence points to problems created by the bureaucratic and monopolistic traits of the school district's "exclusive franchise"[31] in the business of schooling.

Another branch of educational research cited as evidence of the value of school choice comes from studies of private school systems. These studies show that greater parental choice leads to increased parental involvement in all aspects of schooling, creating a more supportive culture for learning.[32] In essence, the values of private choice, parental involvement, and organizational independence are emphasized as incentives to changing the bureaucratic and complex nature of public education.

## Types of Choice

Educational choices can be provided without endorsing market-based choice proposals. Educational historians and scholars have published volumes on the questions surrounding choice in education and to what degree choices are already present in public education. Parents have always been free to choose between schools based on selecting where they live and the neighborhood attendance area; and choosing private schools, which presumably cannot deny children admission. Some have argued that the present system of schooling offers too much choice, where "shopping mall high schools" create a disjointed, undisciplined learning experience.[33]

Because the concept of choice is so broad, it needs to be defined in relation to reform-related values. Raywid outlined four orientations to choice:

> *Education-driven choice*—Provides choices that fit the learning styles of students and the teaching styles of educators. Advocates believe teacher empowerment and school-level autonomy will make education work better and better satisfy the participants.
>
> *Economics-driven choice*—Requires public schools to compete with private schools. Competition, privatization, consumer satisfaction, and markets will put bad schools out of business.
>
> *Policy-driven choice*—Allows for the design of school finance systems that give policy-makers more choice in pursuing educational equity and excellence. Advocates believe policy-driven choices are more advantageous than mandates such as school desegregate orders.
>
> *Governance-driven choice*—Advocates want to remove education from the arena of collective, public decision making and place it in the hands of individuals. To maximize individual choice, students could attend either public or private schools, but the power to decide would be shifted to parents and community members.[34]

These four orientations or approaches to choice have some distinct differences. However they are additive in that they represent a diversity of interests all moving toward the same fundamental political value of private choice.

Choice proposals within public education are not based on a fundamental change in governance, as in Raywid's description of economics-driven choice. At least eight different public choice plans have been identified within the current system.

  1. *Interdistrict open enrollment*—allows parents to send their children to their neighborhood school, another public school in their district, or another public school in a different school district.

  2. *Intradistrict open enrollment*—school choice is limited to public schools within a district.

  3. *Minischools or schools within schools*—educational alternatives are provided within a particular school site.

4. *Magnet Schools*—a limited version of intradistrict open enrollment plans; a school with unique characteristics to serve as a *magnet* to attract a broad range of students from throughout the district.
5. *Post-secondary options*—allows students to take courses at neighboring post-secondary institutions, often instead of attending the last years of high school.
6. *Minivouchers*—available to a limited number of students who are allowed to purchase specific and limited services outside of the resident school system.
7. *Second-chance or continuation schools*—available to students who have dropped out of high school or are likely to drop out; usually schools providing special programs in nontraditional settings.
8. *Private Contractors*—public schools contract out to private firms to provide certain services.[35]

Each of these options presents trade-offs among important organizational and political goals. Depending on local conditions, they provide differing degrees of family choice. However, these options are relatively new in education, and empirical data on their effects on schools and students is limited.

The application of market theories to school systems is based on several assumptions, some of which may not be plausible within environments designed for learning. Comparisons between public and private school settings have been questioned due to the presence of other organizational, cultural, and demographic factors. Much of the evidence on the effects of choice in education is circumstantial. There are studies of how competition affects other public sector operations. Elmore's analysis of health care points to the need to regulate large, complex systems and the importance of an active public role in managing the terms of choice.[36]

Studies of state and local government agencies show how market-like competition can be effective in some instances. Public agencies can *compete* to solve a public problem, such as air pollution, while cooperating to efficiently market air quality options.[37] School choice advocates, however, have yet to clearly identify how competition and cooperation will occur simultaneously. It is clear that changing educational governance from political control to private, market-driven control would fundamentally change the American system of schooling. Experiments promoting new forms of choice within the public educational system are relatively new and limited. Ironically, the biggest concern about market-based school reform is the potential effects of experimentation on students. Failure of a school in the "educational marketplace" is a different matter than failure of a product line. Schools are communities of young people in the most formative years of life.

## CHARTER SCHOOLS

A charter school is a semiautonomous school within the public education system. Charter schools are administered by groups of parents, teachers, and community members operating under a contract or charter agreement with the local board of education. In some states, charter groups can appeal to the state board of education for a charter if they are unable to reach an agreement with the local board. Charter schools are not separate legal entities, completely independent of the school district or the state. They are public schools defined uniquely by their charter. Under a charter system, groups of teachers request funds directly from the school board to carry out specific instructional programs. Charter schools are not restricted by regulations that apply to the school district, except for compliance with the laws, rules, and regulations concerning health, safety, and civil rights. Commonalities of charter school legislation across the states include:

- Charter schools must be nonsectarian, nonreligious, tuition-free, and subject to all federal and state laws regarding discrimination.
- Charter schools must comply with the pupil performance standards of the district within which they are located. If students fail to meet those standards, the school will be held accountable and the charter may be revoked.
- Charter schools are responsible for their own operating budgets and may negotiate with a school district or other party for services, space, equipment, and transportation.[38]

Charter schools are primarily funded with public dollars and are therefore different from market-based schools of choice proposals which are designed to remove schools from state and local governance systems. In essence, charter schools are experiments financed within the public school system. Groups of sponsoring teachers and parents are free to establish site-based approaches to everything from hiring teachers to use of facilities. School budgets are built on per pupil expenditures which reflect the funding pattern in the student's home district. However, charter schools have greater freedom to raise and retain funds from organizations outside the school district.

The idea of chartering independent groups of teachers and parents to foster school reform is closely linked with Minnesota's movement to public school choice in the late 1980s. Ten states passed charter school legislation by 1994 and at least ten more are considering similar proposals in 1995. The charter school concept was included in President Clinton's educational reform proposals in 1993, and legislation providing start-up funding was subsequently introduced in Congress.[39] Several large cities, including Detroit, Philadelphia, Chicago, and Baltimore have organized variations of the charter school concept. Minnesota recently raised its cap on charter schools from eight to twenty, and there are proposals to increase the number of available charters in California and Colorado.

Craig Sauter's continuum of school restructuring and reform approaches places charter schools in the philosophical center, as seen in Figure 6.1.[40]

Given the range of educational reforms being considered in the 1990s, charter schools appear to provide a form of choice palatable to both state and local policy makers. Research conducted by the Education Commission of the States (ECS) indicates that charter schools represent bipartisan political interest.[41] Five of the eight states that passed charter school legislation by 1994 represent bipartisan political agreements. In the other three states, the Democratic party initiated the charter school legislation. This contradicts the view that charter schools only represent Republican interests in schools vouchers and privatization.

Some of the newly established charter schools are designed primarily to achieve specific curricular reforms, while others are more interested in avoiding the requirements and regulations of school districts. However, there is little data available on the impact of the charter approach on student performance or comparisons between the efficiencies of operating charter schools and similar public schools. There are many unknowns about the mechanics of sponsoring and operating charter schools. It is not clear how many charter school advocates have the ability and stamina to operate effective schools once they are established. Although the interest and political support for charter school legislation is diverse and widespread, there are no guarantees that the student composition of newly chartered schools will reflect the long-held American tradition of equal educational opportunity. The recent success of the Edison Project in contracting to operate three charter schools in

| CENTRALIZED ◄─────────────────────────────► DECENTRALIZED | | | | | | |
|---|---|---|---|---|---|---|
| Public Schools | Choice Intradistrict | Choice Interdistrict | **Charter Schools** | Voucher Tax Credit | Private School | Home School |

**FIGURE 6.1  Continuum of Choice Proposals**

Massachusetts sets a precedent for franchise-style schools supported by public dollars.[42] The possibility of federal support for charter school development could create competition and confusion for state and local boards facing severe financial limitations.

Charter schools represent a significant change in educational governance. They will inevitably create complex and unpredictable challenges for state and local school boards. Administrators and board members must develop procedures for reviewing charter proposals within the parameters of state legislation. Governing boards must also consider their redefined legal and regulatory responsibilities along with opportunities to provide contract services to newly chartered schools.

Regardless of the organizers' specific intentions, charter schools have captured bipartisan political support in many states and communities. For an increasing number of educational policy makers, charter schools are a vehicle for teachers, parents, and community members to create a new educational delivery system with public support.

## SCHOOL BOARD REFORM

Whether school board members are elected or appointed, they are officially involved in decision making and allocating resources and authority. Although changes in governance have occurred in the history of public education, the district-based governance system has remained essentially intact since its inception.[43] The first wave of reform in the early 1980s largely overlooked or ignored the conditions of local school boards. Emphasis on restructuring in the second wave has led to increased attention and intense criticism of local governing boards. In a relatively short period of time, site-based management and schools of choice shifted attention to educational governance, which in turn led to greater scrutiny of school boards. Board members themselves complain about their diminishing authority and compromised positions in a complex system of state regulations, unionized teacher contracts, and federal mandates.

Many of these conditions were created by forces outside the control of school districts and their governing boards. Kirst believes district autonomy has been shrinking for several years, due to simultaneous pressures from federal and local interests:[44]

Figure 6.2 shows how local discretion has been squeezed by top-down forces and the bottom-up influence of private groups and reformers. When centralized reforms in the 1990s, such as national goals and performance standards, are combined with decentralizing site-based management interests, local school boards are put in an unstable and unpredictable middle

+ Federal

+ State

+ Courts

+ Interstate networks

+ Private business

---

– School Board

– Local Superintendent

– Local central administration

---

+ Teacher collective bargaining

+ Administrator bargaining

+ Community-based interest groups

---

+ Increasing influence

– Decreasing influence

**FIGURE 6.2    Trends in Educational Governance: 1950–1987**

*Source:* Sergiovanni, Thomas J., and John H. Moore. *Schooling for Tomorrow,* p. 67. Copyright 1989 by Allyn and Bacon. Adapted by permission.

ground. The losers in the governance power shift ultimately will be the local boards and central offices because education has become a national priority.[45] Similar predictions come from site-based governance councils, who are well aware of the problems school boards are facing.

Critics of school board governance point to low levels of participation in local elections and the citizenry's general lack of interest or knowledge of school board functions. Nationwide studies of the conditions of local school boards found that they often:

• Fail to provide far reaching or politically risky leadership for school reform.
• Have become too involved in micromanaging districts.
• Are often splintered by members' attempts to represent special interests or their own individual political interests.
• Pay little attention to their own performance and their needs for ongoing training.[46]

Debates about the degree of change needed in school board governance are driven by different interpretations of democratic participation in education, local control of schools, parental choice, and organizational reforms that emphasize school based and/or national-level decision making. The variety of proposed reforms range along a spectrum from providing training for school boards and fundamentally preserving the status quo to creating totally new local governance structures that would divorce the functions of overall local education policy making from the operation of schools. The Institute for Educational Leadership (IEL) outlined a series of recommendations based on the conditions that have emerged from two waves and ten years of educational reforms and from changes in the electorates' views about governance and political participation.

- Transform local school boards into education policy boards to focus on development, implementation, and oversight of policies that improve the academic achievement of all students.
- Increase the ability of school boards to focus on the pressing policy issues that face public education by relieving them of responsibility for detailed management and budget implementation decisions.
- Require local school boards to play an active role in oversight of the educational process in their districts.
- Strive to change the perceptions and expectations of the citizenry about the appropriate role of local school boards.
- Enable school boards to make the most effective, economical use of existing resources.
- Provide school boards with a flexible framework that allows them to create policies that serve the particular needs of the students and community in their district.[47,76]

In many cases, these objectives require state legislative support, due to legal provisions in which state governments establish the roles, responsibilities, and legal authority of local boards. IEL's report recognizes the need for comprehensive improvement efforts because of the degree of turnover among board members (approximately one third per year as a national average) and the inability of most boards to commit to sustained development. IEL states: "These recommendations . . . call for fundamental change, not just tinkering with what is and enacting piecemeal legislation to deal only with symptoms and not with basic problems."[48]

It can be difficult to determine whether a proposed school board reform will create a fundamental change or no change at all. An attempt to review school board procedures could uncover the need for more dramatic changes, while a proposal to fundamentally change school board elections could result in no change at all. Major changes in school board governance will pose considerable difficulties due to the complex nature of educational governance and the political quality of public decision making.

## STATE GOVERNANCE REFORM

Educational governance at the state level is based upon formal agreements and hierarchical legal structures encompassing several different government organizations and political entities. State boards of education are empowered by the state legislature to make educational policies and implement state-wide programs. State boards of education have not received the attention local boards have faced in the 1990s. Even though the states became more active in school reform, there have been few structural changes in the system of boards, chief state school officers, and departments of education. A study of state education governance structures commissioned in 1993 discovered a trend away from representative governance of education, based on popular elections of state school board members. Several states switched from elections to appointment of board members, particularly by governors. The study found:

- Nine states modified governance structures between 1993 and 1983, representing more centralized approaches to selecting the chief state school officer or state board of education.
- Three of these states authorized the governor to appoint both the state board of education and the chief state school officer.
- The entire state board of education is appointed by the governor in thirty-one states, and part of the board is appointed by the governor in five other states.[49]

The most significant change in recent years has been the centralization of authority to achieve state-wide or nationwide reforms. Through regulatory activities and state-wide mandates, governors, state legislatures, and state departments of education have become more involved in local school issues. One estimate reported that 80 percent of local board policy is the implementation of state education agency and federal regulations and guidelines.[50]

This shift in authority to the state level is an example of how governance changes can be brought about indirectly through reforms directed at other aspects of public education. The increased involvement of state boards, state education agencies, and governors was not a concerted and well-organized structural reform, but the outcome of reforms directed primarily at student performance, graduation requirements, and teaching. Even though there have been few structural changes, a significant shift in authority to state level governing bodies occurred by virtue of enacting system-wide changes.

## PUBLIC AND PRIVATE SECTOR PARTNERSHIPS

Agreements between schools and public and private organizations are generally designed to improve the quality of public education or to improve the efficiency of school systems. Yet collaborative agreements can indirectly but significantly impact governance by including more actors in decision making. Along with agreements to share resources are the need to agree on how those resources will be used. Partnerships consequently require changes in governance that are often secondary considerations. Partnerships allow or encourage public managers and private sector representatives to participate in school or district decision making. Interagency agreements emphasize or mandate closer relations with communities and related public service agencies. Although generally considered a positive change, the inclusion of new actors in educational decision making complicates governance proceedings, with policy makers often representing different levels of knowledge and interest.

A variety of approaches to linking schools with other public and private organizations has emerged in the last few years. Driven in part by the school reform movement and continuing fiscal shortages in public agencies, new program designs and organizational partnerships are available for policy makers, administrators, and scholars to consider. Three broad categories are *school-business partnerships, school-public agency partnerships,* and *school-community partnerships.*

### School-Business Partnerships

School-business partnerships are based on schools entering into agreements with private sector organizations in order to access services, technical assistance, and money.[51] The number of school-business partnerships has steadily increased in the 1980s and 1990s, representing two types of private sector involvement: business round tables and business-education partnerships. Round tables is a term that refers to task forces, forums, or commissions that bring business interests and fundraising to bear on programs and policy decisions. Many of these formal business groups were organized in the 1980s as a reaction to and reflection of state and national interest in educational reform. The most common example of business-education partnerships that are local in origin and impact are adopt-a-school programs.

Whether corporate involvement is national, regional, or school specific, it generally carries assumptions about how schools should change and how interorganizational partnerships should be designed. Business involvement, either at the policy level or in providing resources for specific schools, frequently creates conflict and confusion over school purposes and institutional obstacles. Interorganizational agreements are difficult to establish when schools as public institutions cannot quickly restructure, based on the expectations of corporate managers who are accustomed to greater flexibility and control.

## School-Public Agency Partnerships

Partnerships between schools and public agencies are designed to serve distinct populations or to increase the general level of services in schools. School districts are forming agreements with human service agencies in a movement to provide integrated services or school-linked social services. Human service agencies offer programs such as day care and health services at the school site. Social workers, counselors, job placement officers, and health-care workers operate out of school facilities and interact with teachers and administrators as well as with children and families.

Several forces are at work to initiate school-linked social services. At the policy level, child-centered reforms attempt to focus a variety of public services to better serve children, particularly in urban settings.[52] At the programmatic level, school-linked social services are designed to cut costs, eliminate paperwork, avoid duplication, and improve relations between communities and local schools.

From the perspective of the other public sector partners, operating agreements with schools occur within the context of intergovernmental relations and interagency management.[53] As pointed out in Chapter 4, local school districts, state school boards and state education agencies are units of government and are legally bound by intergovernmental management policies and procedures.

## School-Community Partnerships

School-community partnerships represent a multitude of approaches involving a mix of nonprofit organizations, foundations, businesses, and public agencies in school improvement. School-initiated partnerships with the community include citizens' accountability or review committees and various types of advisory boards and site-based management teams.

Community-initiated partnerships with schools take on more prescriptive characteristics. Created to provide additional resources for schools, they often focus on specific issues and programs and are more likely to test the limits and conditions of interagency cooperation. Denver's Family Resource Schools Project is a descriptive example. Resource Center Schools are managed by site coordinators who attempt to provide services in schools from outside agencies such as social services and public health. The project is governed by an executive committee composed of foundation officers, corporate leaders, and representatives from community groups. Private foundations in the Denver area provide grants to enhance the range of programming and activities offered by public schools in inner-city neighborhoods.[54] One of the biggest obstacles to the project is coordinating services between different public agencies who have different program goals, funding guidelines, and eligibility requirements. Members of the governing board from outside the school system have been both enlightened and frustrated by the barriers to interagency collaboration.

## *Implications of Partnerships and Collaboration*

Based on trends of the last ten years, the number and scope of school-based partnerships will continue to increase. Observers of school reform have noted that school-community collaboration has become a cornerstone of reform in the 1990s.[55] The potential of educational partnerships is significant enough to initiate a shift in the governance of public education, one that could significantly improve the quality of educational services. Partnerships require a more decentralized decision-making structure, which is more flexible and inclusive of business interests, universities, and other social service agencies. Partnerships would not just supplement the activities of schooling but would be built in to governance structures and delivery of educational services.

Partnerships with organizations external to the environment of the schools require both formal agreements and informal working relationships. Educators and private sector managers come from settings with often conflicting values and expectations. Partnerships represent agreements between organizational cultures as well as individuals, and they take time and talent to maintain. As collaborative agreements between agencies become more commonplace, administrators will need to develop skills in interagency management, consensus building, and collaboration.

The dynamics of school-linked social services or integrated services can be complex and challenging. Preliminary studies show that even if integrated services are well planned and interagency agreements are thoughtfully initiated, conditions supporting human services can vary widely and change markedly.[56] The details of program management and implementation often generate unanticipated impacts on services and outcomes.

## SCHOOL FINANCE REFORMS

School finance is a particularly complex and controversial aspect of educational governance. School finance systems include state and local efforts to obtain and allocate public financial support for schools. Thousands of statistical formulas and legal requirements have been established to combine state and local tax revenues and direct them to local districts in ways that are both equitable and efficient. State finance formulas and per-pupil expenditures represent the key outcome of educational governance decisions and the formal record of public values. As a function of governance, finance decisions represent a series of economic and political compromises that directly affect all aspects of education.

School finance systems are increasingly being used as avenues to school reform. Funding formulas can be redesigned to more closely link educational costs to achieving reform goals.[57] Attempts to implement new teacher compensation systems, site-based management plans, outcome-based performance standards, and schools of choice all require significant changes in school finance. Modifications in finance and budgeting procedures often represent significant changes in state and local governance because they require a shift in authority over financial decisions. School-level management teams need the ability to direct resources to locally established goals and programs. However, significant changes in budget allocations and spending patterns require the authority of governing boards at the district and/or state level. Many reforms directed at decentralization have overlooked the complex, intergovernmental nature of school finance and the difficulty of changing state finance policies and procedures.

State-level finance reforms can radically alter local governance patterns. Kentucky's Education Reform Act of 1990 was largely a result of litigation directed at the inequities of the state school finance formula. Yet the Act mandated school-based management along with a state curriculum framework and a performance-based student assessment program.[58] In 1992, school finance structures in twenty-six states were being debated in the courts, generally due to questions of fiscal inequities and challenges over the equality of educational opportunities. The results of legal decisions will continue to impact state and local governance, demonstrating the close link between financial resources and educational decision making. Wohlstetter and Buffet quote a school superintendent to summarize the relationship between school finance and governance: "It's the 'golden rule': whoever has the gold rules."[59]

School finance disputes are producing new governance issues for state and local policy makers. Due to shortfalls in state and local property tax support, failed bond initiatives, rising costs, and other factors, state legislatures and local districts are increasingly pursuing financial support from sources other than the traditional reliance on property taxes. In 1994, the Michigan Legislature voted to repeal the state's property tax system for financing schools in favor of a mix of sales taxes and other business tax revenues.[60] Increasing tax revenues from business and industry sources intensifies the degree of scrutiny from those organizations and their interest groups. The adage "He who pays the piper picks the tune" suggests that new funding streams come with strings attached.

In Colorado, several school districts in the Denver metropolitan area have imposed impact fees on new residential development through the taxing authority of county governments. Political controversies are escalating as school districts are viewed by other units of local government as competitors for limited public revenues.[61] Developers are increasingly criticizing school governance decisions because they feel they are paying a greater share of the cost of education, without adequate justification for present spending patterns.

Any significant changes in school finance will affect state and local governance. The search for alternative revenues directly or inadvertently brings new participants into educational decision making. The challenge for educational policy makers is to coordinate finance and governance changes in ways that support more effective and efficient decision making.

## THE CUMULATIVE EFFECTS OF SCHOOL REFORM ON EDUCATIONAL GOVERNANCE

Ten years of school reform has generated greater interest and closer scrutiny of educational governance, from the local school level to the national debate about goals and standards. Initiatives generated by an increasing diversity of organizations and interest groups create a system-wide sense of uncertainty and unpredictability that leaves little doubt that educational governance will undergo significant change. Reform initiatives including decentralization, national goals, schools of choice, and charter schools are based on the premise that the system itself must change. Early indications of the cumulative effects of these reforms are unsettling for local governing boards. Decentralization and national goals put district governing boards in an unstable, middle ground. Growing interest in public school choice and charter schools suggests semiautonomous, publicly funded schooling could replace more traditional district systems over time.

Although many proposed governance changes are outcomes of the restructuring movement and the second wave of reform in the late 1980s, the environment for educational change in the 1990s is different from the spirit of restructuring. Restructuring implies doing something different with the existing structure. As Kolderie states: "'Restructuring' improves on the old prescription: higher salaries, smaller classes and better training. But as it stands it does not got to the heart of the problem. It is trying to persuade districts to change, while accepting as 'given' the system of public education that makes it hard for them to change. This makes no basic sense. It would be better to examine the 'givens' of the system, find what makes it so hard to change, and change that." [62]

What began as restructuring appears to be evolving into a new era of reform that has yet to be defined. This new era was predicted by the dramatic appeals of advocates of the restructuring movement. In 1990, Richard Elmore pointed to the "potentially powerful coincidence of political, business, professional, and academic interests that could dramatically affect public education if they were to act in concert."[63] This prediction appears to be coming true.

Governance reforms are fundamentally political, involving shifts in authority and changes in the process of decision making. They involve a broader group of stakeholders and interest groups from past efforts to improve teaching and learning. Consequently, the specific focus and impacts of change are hard to predict. However, the desire for change is pervasive and premised on the need to do more than restructure elements in the existing system. School reform in the 1990s is less about *re*-structuring and *re*-forming the existing system than it is about creating a new system of school sponsorship and control.

## SUMMARY

The first and second waves of school reform in the 1980s and early 1990s have produced both direct and indirect challenges to educational governance. Attention to organizational and system-wide aspects of schooling in the second wave focused greater attention on restructuring governance systems by realigning patterns of authority.

Decentralization in education is an attempt to redistribute authority to school sites and localized decision-making groups. Decentralization is a primary goal and political strategy in most restructuring plans, despite several implementation issues and the lack of evidence of positive effects on student performance.

Centralization is manifested in national education goals and efforts to establish nationwide performance standards and curricula. Greater centralization of educational decision making has occurred as a result of national and state-wide reforms in the past ten years.

Balancing the forces of decentralization and centralization is a critical issue for educational policy makers. Even though the present system of public education is the result of a series of practical compromises between national interests and the American tradition of local control, debates between decentralization and centralization of educational governance are likely to continue.

Choice-driven school reforms consistently emphasize the role of parents in controlling the selection of schools for their children. There are a variety of ways to enhance choice within the public school setting, as well as proposals to create market-based systems for selecting schools. However, concerns remain about the lack of evidence of the benefits of school choice for students and the consequences of the failure of any school in the educational marketplace.

Charter schools are semiautonomous schools within the public education system. Funded primarily with public dollars, charter schools are different from market-based schools of choice which would remove schools from local governance systems. Given the range of educational reforms being considered in the 1990s, charter schools appear to be a form of choice acceptable to many state and local policy makers.

School board reforms represent efforts to improve or redesign formal governance structures. Local school boards appear to be losing their authority and discretion to national, state, and local entities. Many important school board reforms require legal and political support from state governments, demonstrating the complex, intergovernmental nature of educational governance. Changes in state level governance are more the result of informal shifts of decision-making authority to carry out other types of school reform than they are representative of formal, structural changes in governance systems.

Public and private sector partnerships are based on agreements between schools and external organizations to improve the quality of public education or to improve the efficiency of school systems. Collaborative agreements with public and private organizations can indirectly but significantly impact school governance by including new participants in decision making.

State finance formulas and local per-pupil spending patterns represent key outcomes of educational governance decisions. School finance systems are increasingly being used as avenues to school reform. State level finance reform and litigation can significantly alter local governance patterns. Alternative sources of funding for schools bring new participants into educational governance, as well as greater scrutiny of school spending and decision making.

Ten years of school reform has led to greater interest in educational management and governance. Initiatives such as decentralization and schools of choice require fundamental change, resulting in a cumulative effect of unpredictability and uncertainty. School reform in the 1990s is less about *re*-structuring and *re*-forming the existing system than it is about creating a new system of school sponsorship and control.

## SEMINAR QUESTIONS

1. Should school reform emphasize greater decentralization or centralization of decision making? Do you think these two approaches can occur simultaneously?

2. Can the existing system of public education support greater school choice? If so, how?

3. Will charter schools create equal educational opportunities?

4. Do you believe we are entering a new era of school reform in the 1990s? If so, how could it be described or characterized?

## SUGGESTED READINGS

Clune, William H. and John F. Witte, eds. *Choice and Control in American Education.* Vol.1. New York: Falmer Press, 1990.

Elmore, Richard F., ed. *Restructuring Schools: The Next Generation of Educational Reform.* San Francisco: Jossey-Bass, 1990.

Hannaway, Jane and Martin Carnoy, eds. *Decentralization and School Improvement.* San Francisco: Jossey-Bass, 1991.

Odden, Allan R., ed. *Rethinking School Finance: An Agenda for the 1990s.* San Francisco: Jossey-Bass, 1992.

Sergiovanni, Thomas J. and John H. Moore, eds. *Schooling for Tomorrow: Directing Reforms to Issues That Count.* Boston: Allyn & Bacon, 1989.

## ENDNOTES

1. *A Nation at Risk: The Imperative for Educational Reform* (Washington, DC: Commission on Excellence in Education, U.S. Government Printing Office, 1983).
2. Larry Cuban, "Reforming Again, Again, and Again," *Educational Researcher,* (Washington, DC: American Educational Research Association, January 1990). Also see Kenneth A. Sirotnik, "The School as the Center of Change," in *Schooling for Tomorrow: Directing Reforms to Issues That Count,* ed. Thomas J. Sergiovanni and John H. Moore (Boston: Allyn & Bacon, 1989), p. 97.
3. Education Commission of the States, *Restructuring the Education System: A Consumer's Guide* (Denver: Education Commission of the States, 1991). *Restructuring Schools: The Next Generation of Educational Reform,* ed. Richard F. Elmore (San Francisco: Jossey-Bass, 1990), pp. 1–28.
4. Martha McCarthy, *State Education Governance Structures* (Denver Education Commission of the States, November 1993), p. 2.
5. Michael Cohen, "Key Issues Confronting State Policy Makers," in *Restructuring Schools: The Next Generation of Educational Reform,* ed. Richard F. Elmore (San Francisco: Jossey-Bass, 1990), p. 251.
6. Kenneth A. Sirotnik, "The School as the Center of Change," in *Schooling for Tomorrow: Directing Reforms to Issues That Count,* ed. Thomas J. Sergiovanni and John H. Moore (Boston: Allyn & Bacon, 1989), p. 97. Also see Dennis Doyle, "Business-Led School Reform: The Second Wave," *Across the Board* (November 1987).
7. Carl D. Glickman, "Pushing School Reform to a New Edge: The Seven Ironies of School Empowerment," *Phi Delta Kappan* (September 1990), p. 69.
8. Jacqueline P. Danzberger, "Governing the Nation's Schools: The Case for Restructuring Local School Boards," *Phi Delta Kappan* (January 1994), pp. 367–373.
9. Daniel Oran and Jay M. Shafritz, *The MBA's Dictionary* (Reston, Va.: Reston Publishing, 1983), p. 121.
10. Glickman, "Pushing School Reform to a New Edge: The Seven Ironies of School Empowerment," *Phi Delta Kappan* (September 1990).
11. Lisa Carlos and Mary Amsler, "Site-Based Management: An Experiment in Governance," *Policy Briefs,* no. 20. (San Francisco: Far West Laboratory, 1993), p. 2.
12. Hans N. Weiler, "Comparative Perspectives on Educational Decentralization: An Exercise in Contradiction," *Educational Evaluation and Policy Analysis,* vol. 12, no. 4 (Winter 1990), pp. 433–448. Also see Hans N. Weiler, "Control Versus Legitimation: The Politics of Ambivalence," in *Decentralization and School Improvement,* ed. Jane Hannaway and Martin Carnoy (San Francisco: Jossey-Bass, 1991), pp. 55–83.
13. Richard F. Elmore, *Education and Federalism: Doctrinal, Functional, and Strategic Views,* project reports no. 83–A13 (Stanford University: Institute for Research on Educational Finance and Governance, 1983). Also see Thomas

R. Dye, *American Federalism: Competition Among Governments* (Lexington: Lexington Books, 1990).

14. Colleen A. Capper and Michael T. Jamison, "Let the Buyer Beware: Total Quality Management and Educational Research and Practice," *Educational Researcher,* vol. 22 (November 1993), pp. 25–30.

15. David E. Osborne and Ted Gaebler, *Reinventing Government: How the Entrepreneurial Spirit is Transforming the Public Sector,* (Reading, Mass.: Addison-Wesley, 1992).

16. Janet Weiss, "Control in School Organizations: Theoretical Perspectives," in *Choice and Control in American Education,* vol. 1, ed. William H. Clune and John F. Witte (New York: Falmer Press, 1990), p. 125.

17. Michael Fullan, *The Meaning of Educational Change,* 2nd ed. (New York: Teachers College Press, 1991). Also see Carl L. Marburger, *One School at a Time: School Based Management, A Process for Change* (Columbia: National Committee for Citizens in Education, 1989).

18. Priscilla Wohlstetter and Thomas M. Buffett, "Promoting School-Based Management: Are Dollars Decentralized Too?" in *Rethinking School Finance: An Agenda for the 1990s,* ed. Allan R. Odden (San Francisco: Jossey-Bass, 1992), p. 159.

19. Richard F. Elmore, "School Decentralization: Who Gains? Who Loses?" In *Decentralization and School Improvement,* ed. Jane Hannaway and Martin Carnoy (San Francisco: Jossey-Bass, 1993), pp. 44–45.

20. Ulrich C. Reitzug, "Self-Managed Leadership: An Alternative School Governance Structure," *The Urban Review,* vol. 24, no. 2 (1992), pp. 133–147.

21. Glickman, "Pushing School Reform to a New Edge: The Seven Ironies of School Impowerment," p. 69.

22. Allan R. Odden and Lori Kim, "Reducing Disparities across the States: A New Federal Role in School Finance," in *Rethinking School Finance: An Agenda for the 1990s,* ed. Allan R. Odden (San Francisco: Jossey-Bass, 1992), pp. 260–261.

23. Lester Thurow, *Head to Head: The Coming Economic Battle Among Japan, Europe, and America* (New York: William Morrow, 1992), p. 259.

24. John L. Keedy, "The Twin Engines of School Reform for the 1990s: The School Sites and National Coalitions," *Journal of School Leadership,* vol. 4, no. 1 (January 1994) pp. 94–111. Keedy reports that when national performance standards are emphasized, it appears that most voters are willing to accept a more centralized educational system. In 1991, 81 percent of Americans surveyed favored requiring public schools in their communities to conform to national achievement standards and goals. Perhaps more significantly, 68 percent favored a standardized national curriculum.

25. Michael Cohen, *Results in Education: Restructuring the Education System,* (Washington, DC: National Governors' Association, Center for Policy Research, 1988), p. 19.

26. Paul Peterson, "Monopoly and Competition in American Education," in William H. Clune and John F. Witte, eds., *Choice and Control in American Education* (New York: Falmer Press, 1990), pp. 47–78.

27. Elmore, "School Decentralization: Who Gains? Who Loses?" p. 52.

28. William L. Boyd, "Public Education's Last Hurrah? Schizophrenia, Amnesia, and Ignorance in School Politics." *Educational Evaluation and Policy Analysis,* vol. 9 (1987), pp. 85–100.
29. Mary A. Raywid, "Rethinking School Governance," in *Restructuring Schools: The Next Generation of Educational Reform,* ed. Richard F. Elmore (San Francisco: Jossey-Bass, 1990). Also see *Policy Guide: A State Policy Maker's Guide to Public School Choice,* Denver Education Commission of the States, (1989).
30. David Hogan, ". . . the Silent Compulsions of Economic Relations: Markets and the Demand for Education," *Educational Policy,* vol. 6 (June 1992), pp. 180–205. Also see William L. Boyd, "The Power of Paradigms: Reconceptualizing Educational Policy and Management," *Educational Administration Quarterly,* vol. 28, no. 4 (November 1992), pp. 504–528. Also see Henry M. Levin, *The Theory of Choice Applied to Education* (Stanford, Calif.: Stanford University, Center for Educational Research, 1989).
31. Ted Kolderie, "The States Must Withdraw the Exclusive Franchise," *National Civic Review,* vol. 80 (1991), p. 52.
32. Anthony S. Bryk, Valerie E. Lee and Julia B. Smith, "High School Organization and Its Effects on Teachers and Students: An Interpretive Summary of the Research," in *Choice and Control in American Education,* vol. 1, ed. William H. Clune and John F. Witte (New York: Falmer, 1990), pp. 135–226. Also see Chubb and Moe, *Politics, Markets, and America's Schools.*
33. Arthur G. Powell, E. Farrar and D. K. Cohen. *The Shopping Mall High School: Winners and Losers in the Educational Market Place* (New York: Houghton Mifflin, 1985).
34. Mary A. Raywid, "Choice Orientations, Discussions, and Prospects," *Educational Policy,* vol. 6, no. 2 (1992), p. 114.
35. Allen R. Odden and Nancy Kotowsi, "Financing Public School Choice: Policy Issues and Options," in *Rethinking School Finance: An Agenda for the 1990s,* ed. Allan R. Odden (San Francisco: Jossey-Bass, 1992), pp. 227.
36. Richard Elmore, "Choice as an Instrument of Public Policy: Evidence from Education and Health Care," in *Choice and Control in American Education,* vol. 1, ed. William H. Clune and John F. Witte (New York: Falmer, 1990), p. 314.
37. *Competition Among States and Local Governments,* eds. Daphne A. Kenyon and John Kincaid (Washington, DC: Urban Institute Press, 1991).
38. Paul Bauman, Debra Banks, Michael Murphy and Hal Kuczwara, "The Charter School Movement: Preliminary Findings from the First Three States," unpublished paper presented at the American Educational Research Association Annual Conference (New Orleans, La.: April 1994), pp. 1–31.
39. Kolderie, "The States Must Withdraw the Exclusive Franchise," p. 52. Also see Ray Budde "Educating By Charter," *Phi Delta Kappan,* vol. 70, no. 7, (1989), p. 518–520. *Mandate for Change,* eds. William Marshall and Martin Schram, (New York, NY: Progressive Policy Institute: Barkley Books, 1993).
40. Craig R. Sauter, *Charter Schools: A New Breed of Public Schools.* (Oak Brook Ill.: The North Central Regional Educational Laboratory, 1993).
41. Chris Pipho, "Bipartisan Charter Schools," *Phi Delta Kappan,* vol. 75, no. 3 (1993), p. 102.

42. Mark Walsh, "3 Edison Plans Win Charter-School Backing in Mass.," *Education Week,* (March 23, 1994), p. 13.

43. Jacqueline P. Danzberger, Michael W. Kirst, and Michael D. Usdan, *Governing Public Schools: New Times, New Requirements* (Washington, DC: Institute for Educational Leadership, 1992).

44. Michael W. Kirst, "Who Should Control the Schools? Reassessing Current Policies," in *Schooling for Tomorrow: Directing Reforms to Issues That Count,* ed. Thomas J. Sergiovanni and John H. Moore (Boston: Allyn & Bacon, 1989), pp. 62–88.

45. John L. Keedy, "The Twin Engines of School Reform for the 1990s: The School Sites and National Coalitions," *Journal of School Leadership,* vol. 4 (January 1994), p. 103.

46. Jacqueline P. Danzberger, "Governing the Nation's Schools: The Case for Restructuring Local School Boards," *Phi Delta Kappan* (January 1994), p. 369.

47. The Institute for Educational Leadership, Inc., *Supporting Leaders for Tomorrow: A Framework for Redefining the Role and Responsibilities of Local School Boards* (Washington, DC: September 1993), p. 5.

48. *Supporting Leaders for Tomorrow: A Framework for Redefining the Role and Responsibilities of Local School Boards,* p. 2.

49. Martha McCarthy, *State Education Governance Structures,* (Denver Education Commission of the States, November 1993), p. ix.

50. John L. Keedy, "The Twin Engines of School Reform for the 1990s: The School Sites and National Coalitions," *Journal of School Leadership,* vol. 4, no. 1 (January 1994), pp. 94–111. Also see D. R. Davies, *Education, Democracy, and a New Elitism.* (Bisbee, Ark.: The Bisbee Foundation, 1988).

51. C. Kent McGuire, "Business Involvement in Education in the 1990s," in *Education Politics for the New Century,* ed. D. E. Mitchell and M. E. Goertz (New York: Falmer Press, 1990).

52. Richard A. King and C. Kent McGuire, "Political and Financial Support for School-Based and Child-Centered Reforms," in *The Politics of Urban Education in the United States,* ed. James G. Cibulka, Rodney J. Reed, and Kenneth K. Wong (Washington, DC: Falmer Press, 1991).

53. The intergovernmental relations literature consistently includes public education as a participant. See Deil S. Wright, "Conclusion: Federalism, Intergovernmental Relations, and Intergovernmental Management— Conceptual Reflections, Comparisons, and Interpretations," in *Strategies for Managing Intergovernmental Polities and Networks,* ed. R. W. Gave and M. P. Mandell (New York: Praeger, 1990). However, the role and political position of public education in relation to other levels and functions of government has long been unclear. Research and writings on federalism have described the dynamics of federal aid to education and the impact of block grants in the 1980s. However, there have been few, if any, systematic or theoretical studies of intergovernmental relations or intergovernmental management in education. See Deil S. Wright, *Understanding Intergovernmental Relations* (North Scituate Mass.: Duxbury Press, 1978).

54. *Family Resource Schools* (Denver: Denver Public Schools, 1992), p. 2.
55. Robert L. Crowson and William L. Boyd, "Coordinated Services for Children: Designing Arks for Storms and Seas Unknown," *American Journal of Education,* vol. 101, no. 2 (1993), pp. 140–179. Patrick F. Galvin, "School-Business-University Collaboratives: The Economics of Organizational Choice," unpublished paper presented at the American Educational Research Association (AERA) Conference (New Orleans: April 8, 1994), p. 2.
56. Gary A. Arthur and Paul Bauman, "School-Based Community Services: A Study of Public Agency Partnerships," *Journal of School Leadership* (November 1994) vol. 4, pps. 649–671. Also see Robert E. Behrman, *The Future of Children* (Fullerton Calif.: Center for the Study of Children, 1992).
57. Allen R. Odden, "School Finance in the 1990s," *Phi Delta Kappan* (February 1992).
58. Priscilla Wohlstetter and Thomas M. Buffett, "Promoting School-Based Management: Are Dollars Decentralized Too?" in *Rethinking School Finance: An Agenda for the 1990s,* ed. Allan R. Odden (San Francisco: Jossey-Bass, 1992), pp. 128–165.
59. Wohlstetter and Buffet, "Promoting School-Based Management: Are Dollars Decentralized Too? p. 130–131.
60. David N. Plank, "Slouching Towards Kalkaska," *Politics of Education Bulletin,* (Eugene, Ore.: ERIC Clearinghouse on Educational Management, Winter 1994): vol. 20, p. 6–7.
61. Arthur C. Nelson, *Development Impact Fees: Policy Rationale, Practice, Theory, and Issues* (Chicago: Planners Press, 1989).
62. Ted Kolderie, "The States Must Withdraw the Exclusive Franchise," *National Civic Review,* vol. 80 (1991), p. 52.
63. Richard F. Elmore "Introduction: On Changing the Structure of Public Schools," in *Restructuring Schools: The Next Generation of Educational Reform,* ed. Richard F. Elmore (San Francisco: Jossey-Bass, 1990).

# 7

# GOVERNANCE SKILLS

*We need to develop an image of positive politics*
*and of the manager as constructive politician.*
—Bolman and Deal in
*Reframing Organizations*

Effective participation in governance requires a combination of factual knowledge and interpersonal abilities. Governance skills can be viewed as applied political knowledge, similar to practicing a craft. Like a craft, political skills are exercised in highly personal ways, through intuition, initiative, patience, and thoughtfulness. Becoming effective in governance settings requires some explicit knowledge about public policies and experience in public decision making. Learning cannot be limited to personal experience because many governing environments are poor models of democratic decision making. Preparation for governance in the political environment of the 1990s cannot be left to chance.

Governance skills involve ways of thinking as much as technical approaches to completing specific tasks. Policy making and administration require thinking about democratic participation in constructive and practical ways. By definition, democracy seeks the widest possible level of involvement in decision making, including students, parents, community members, and educators. With the emergence of site-based management and reforms designed to decentralize decision making, the practice of governance will require new approaches to public participation. Mediation and conflict management are as important as the many technical requirements associated with managing large organizations. In order to provide a complete picture of educational leadership, this chapter includes an inventory of traditional administrative skills, as well as a review of the political skills necessary in the changing environment of educational governance.

## THE CONTEXT OF EDUCATIONAL ADMINISTRATION

Many governance settings are relatively chaotic. Uncertainty and a sense of disorder are common. Administrators quickly find themselves in the middle of conflicts and are prone to crisis management. It takes a high level of maturity and patience to be proactive rather than reactive to issues that are posed as major crises. Previous chapters have identified many of the factors that generate these conditions. Continuous waves of school reform and overlapping levels of government combine to create a sense of complexity and confusion. Pressure groups and divided parent communities are common in large and small school districts. Sergiovanni's description of the principalship as "managing messes"[1] is probably more accurate than thinking about school administration as a logical process of problem solving and applying standard managerial techniques.

Becoming skillful in this kind of environment is a formidable challenge. Thinking of ways to create less autocratic and more democratic learning environments is intellectually and physically demanding. However, there is room for optimism. Constructive and collaborative forms of decision making often emerge from people who are thoughtful about educational policies and administrative practices. Administrators can learn a great deal from these settings. Learning about governance experientially as well as in traditional content terms has significant implications for the preparation of school leaders. The emphasis shifts from solving problems to the ability to reflect on the sometimes subtle, sometimes disruptive aspects of politics, authority, and control. Being reflective and thoughtful means that one does not make quick assumptions about the norms and values in a school. Thoughtfulness requires listening and being suspicious of easy answers to complex problems.

There is a tendency among many administrators to take action and "get something done," particularly when the public is calling for visible and immediate school improvements. As Carl Glickman states: "I'm wary of school people's impulse to jump on the restructuring bandwagon without assessing their own readiness to take on the pain and to confront the conflicts involved—and without realizing the extraordinary courage necessary to sustain such change."[2] Administrative actions can be antithetical to longer, more demanding approaches to group decision making. Ironically, governance participants must be careful about their desire to govern. School governance committees often merely attend meetings in which principals or superintendents establish the agenda, make judgments concerning the acceptability of any related discussion, and reserve the right to make final decisions. This approach is no more empowering to professional staff than the autocratic mandates of the past.[3]

## STRATEGIC THINKING

Strategic thinking is an awareness of important organizational goals combined with an appreciation of the consequences of administrative decisions. Being strategic involves a high level of political savvy and insight. Effectively managing political environments requires the use of data to make better decisions while constantly assessing the impact of short- and long-term policies. Strategic planning is a useful method for sorting out political environments. Designed to accommodate the complexities of public organizations, strategic planning and management differ from administrative approaches that assume organizations are rationally designed and tightly controlled. Practices such as management by objectives often ignore or try to circumvent the political nature of life in public agencies. Strategic planning is an inductive process involving the preparation of background reports on external and internal forces and trends. A strategic scan of the environment produces a management information system that can be used to assess an organization's strengths and weaknesses in dealing with critical political issues.

Table 7.1 lists critical factors in the educational environment.[4] These factors represent the many considerations that in one way or another influence what schools are, what they do, and how they behave as organizations. These factors represent both internal and external forces for designing effective planning and decision-making systems.

Educational administrators are increasingly relying on strategic planning approaches to explore the implications of their decisions. Other methods from policy analysis and political science help determine the presence of sometimes subtle forces from the social, political, and economic environment. These methods often require large-scale information gathering and data analysis. Advances in computer technology and inexpensive commercial applications allow even small school systems to benefit from analytical approaches that consider large amounts of quantitative and qualitative data. Advocates of strategic planning emphasize the importance of data collection methods that facilitate democratic communication

**TABLE 7.1    Critical Factors in Educational Environments**

| | |
|---|---|
| Governmental | Legislation, regulations, reporting requirements<br>Political issues, e.g. funding, accountability, certification<br>School board elections/appointments<br>Power shifts from one party to another, funding sources, special programs, social priorities |
| Demographics | Number and characteristics of families and students<br>Characteristics of school personnel<br>Population shifts, in/out migration<br>Cultural traditions and values |
| Organizational Culture | Values, traditions |
| Perceptions of School's Goals | Teachers, parents, students, administrators, staff |
| Interaction with Community | School board relationships<br>Utilization of agency expertise<br>Utilization of human resources<br>Extremist views |
| Economic | Health of local, state, and national economies<br>Consumer preferences and trends<br>Shifting sources of revenue to/from local or state sources |
| Technological | Job requirements, changing communication needs and patterns<br>Home-school linkages via technology<br>Developing breakthroughs in technology and means to access information<br>Pressures to acquire new technology for instruction<br>Changes in work environment |

and participation, while accommodating divergent interests and values. Comprehensive listings of environmental factors help busy policy makers and administrators recognize the implications and consequences of governance decisions. They can also be used to explain the depth and breadth of school systems as social organizations to policy makers and community members who are expecting rapid change.

## *Technical Skills Inventory*

The technical knowledge relevant to educational governance can be viewed as part of the knowledge base that supports the profession and practice of educational administration. School- and district-level administrators complete course work in two broad domains of knowledge. The first is generally referred to as the core technology of education and the second is the knowledge base associated with administration and management.

The core technology of education refers to the many theories and methods that explain how students learn and how teachers teach. Teaching and learning as areas of study are further organized around knowledge from other fields in the behavioral sciences and specialties within education. The core technology of education includes curriculum development, understanding of group process, and knowledge of the social and educational values underlying educational decisions. Table 7.2 lists the core technology recommended for principals by the National Policy Board for Educational Administration.[5]

Research shows that effective school leaders give prime attention to a school's core technology. The literature on superintendents and principals as instructional leaders supports the view that administrators must be familiar with and preferably experienced in the enterprise of teaching and learning.

Descriptions of educational administration as a field of knowledge also include virtually all the expectations associated with management in the private sector and in public agencies. As in private sector management, the historical emphasis in educational administration is technical and scientific.[6] Professional tenets in education are derived from requirements in other administrative fields. A strong commitment to the values and language of administrative science is consistent with broader norms in the social sciences and private industry. A contemporary listing of administrative requirements is basically the same as what was proposed in 1937 and restated in 1955 by the American Association of School Administrators.[7] These lists include planning, organizing, staffing, directing, coordinating, and budgeting. In addition to the skills required to complete these tasks, administrators are expected to be knowledgeable about legal and regulatory issues in education. They are also expected to understand the fundamentals of school finance. As participants in governance, administrators must also have some familiarity with the policy-making process described in Chapter 2.

Awareness of the professional expectations of school administrators is helpful for prospective school leaders, as well as for lay members of gov-

**TABLE 7.2  The Core Technology in Educational Administration**

Instruction and the Learning Environment
Curriculum Design
Student Guidance and Development
Staff Development
Measurement and Evaluation
Resource Allocation

erning boards. Realistically, individuals need to prioritize skill requirements and focus on the essentials. The environment in most schools, district offices, and state agencies also requires a high level of political competence.

## POLITICAL SAVVY

Politics is the art and science of using influence, authority, and power to achieve important goals. Political skills, like technical skills, are tools for getting things done. However, good technical performance in and of itself isn't always enough to ensure organizational success. Political skills are necessary to balance the multiple demands of complex public organizations. Politics is a process of social influence with the potential of being functional or dysfunctional, with major benefits and risks. Political skill can advance careers and increase personal power. It can also improve communications and the effectiveness and efficiency of organizations.

The first step in developing political skills is getting beyond the negative image of politics. Often associated with corruption, deceit, and unethical behavior, politics congers up negative images of secret meetings, self-serving politicians, and the abuse of the public trust. Educators often have difficulty discussing politics because of their mistrust of both its ends and means. The political nature of education may be obvious to experienced administrators and policy makers; but they may still think of *politics* in adversarial terms. Educators frequently complain about organizational politics, blame state and local policy makers, and wish for conflict-free settings in which politics is unnecessary. Power is also seen as a dangerous and discomforting force in organizations. People who have it deny it; people who want it do not want to appear to hunger for it; and people who engage in its machinations do so secretly.[8] Yet power and politics are inseparable.

Insights from anthropology to organizational psychology offer theories about the ambivalence associated with personal power and organizational politics. Aversion to politics prohibits people from participating in political action and the exchange of power, which intensifies their sense of powerlessness and disdain for politics. Loathing politics induces a self-blindness that creates a dependency on leaders and a debilitating fear of recognizing the pervasiveness of politics in the organization.[9]

Politics cannot be eliminated from organizational life. As parents become involved in school reform, they cannot avoid political questions nor should they pretend that issues of power and authority can be kept out of education. Teachers and administrators who become cynical about the policy process risk being left out of major governance changes. They also risk becoming misinformed about their communities' evolving political values. Reforms such as privatization and site-based management require the input of those who will be most affected. School-level educators have long been insulated from the effects of reform movements due in part to their disdain for politics and the bureaucratic tradition of political neutrality and professional objectivity.

Despite these challenges, the positive side of politics in educational administration is beginning to take shape. Recent studies show that effective administrators are those with well developed political skills.[10] Research in organizational politics and school leadership acknowledges the importance of symbolic and political factors in education, particularly school systems that are plagued by uncertainty and complexity.[11] Many administrators have learned new ways to manage political conflicts by accepting their roles as negotiators and mediators. Political skills are developed through real life experiences in conflict-laden environments, which helps explain why recent graduates of administration programs report that real learning begins on the job. Recognizing this mismatch between job-related skill requirements and traditional approaches to teaching, graduate programs in some states are starting to emphasize problem-based learning, coaching, and other forms of skills-based education.[12]

Regardless of the approach to learning about administration, prospective school leaders must first accept the political nature of education and define political skills in constructive and practical ways. Future participants in governance can begin to identify their strengths and weaknesses in relation to the following aspects of organizational politics.

## Building a Power Base

Building a power base is a fundamental skill in school systems, particularly those divided by competing interest groups. A power base is a working coalition of people, ideas, and physical resources. Shared values and a common vision are critical components of a power base within a school or school system. Externally, powerful coalitions can be developed by school leaders who form partnerships with community groups and businesses. In an era of changing governance, public education will have to build much broader political coalitions with other groups. Schools must break out of their parochialism and recognize the political reality of these new constituencies and work with them.[13]

Effective governance participants have learned to accept the intensity and dynamics of political power, without losing sight of the importance of sharing power. The term *empowerment* has come to represent a more palatable view of politics and power. An empowered group is another way of describing a power base. Empowerment is a recognition and understanding that power and authority are necessary for positive school reform. As Ernesto Cortes states: "We have to live in the world as it is; and we have to understand power."[14]

A comprehensive study of school principals concluded that successful school leaders functioned as forceful and dynamic individuals who brought to their practice high energy, initiative, and a practical stance toward life, among other things.[15] Adjectives such as these are associated with personal power and political savvy. The official position of an administrator is a key factor in defining power. Power is also a function of informal factors. Highly successful political actors rely on spontaneous and strategic social interactions along with formal channels of authority. Social adeptness includes such subjective qualities as general appearance, poise under pressure, temperament, etiquette, self-confidence, and sensitivity. Becoming political often requires being assertive and ambitious and at the same time being sensitive enough to assess social situations and remain silent.

## Interpersonal and Organizational Communications

Communication is the central educational skill. Nearly all things educators do involve oral or written communication. Skill in the exchange of information depends largely on well-developed cognitive abilities and careful use of language. Research shows that school leaders who are effective at initiating change communicate frequently and effectively with individuals and groups. They also facilitate communications among others. Outstanding administrators spend more time communicating as facilitators, providing information and feedback between a diversity of organizational and community representatives.

> *An examination of the research suggests that skilled communicators are effective both in advocacy and inquiry. As advocates, they are able to present information about themselves and others. They are able to espouse their own opinions and provide critical feedback in a way that does not antagonize the listeners. They are also skilled in inquiry, the process of coming to understand the views, needs, and feelings of others. They are careful listeners. Perhaps because of these skills, they are also skilled in group process and are able to engage others in collaborative problem analysis and decision-making.*[16]

Listening skills are essential for gathering information about a school's culture. In situations of scarce resources, listening is often the only thing an administrator can do. Administrative communications include messages in evermore complex and numerous communication networks. Communications include giving or exchanging information, signals, or messages through talk, writing, gestures, electronic impulses, graphics and other forms of expression. Skills associated with organizational communications include the ability to formulate and implement policies related to the exchange of information. School and system-wide policies range from media relations to managing electronic communication systems to the curricular implications of instructional technology.

Astute administrators and effective governance committees understand the power of the press and the importance of public information in school-community relations. They also utilize recent advances in information technologies while recognizing their impacts on students and schools. Technological change in the workplace and the dynamic quality of the information age underscore the importance of information and computer literacy as requisite communication skills.

## *Persuasion*

Persuasion is at the heart of political discourse. Persuasion is the ability to get someone to agree with you who disagrees or does not yet agree with your point of view. Persuasive power enables administrators and policy makers to mobilize people and resources in the process of building alliances and political support.

There is nothing inherently wrong with persuasion and believing that your position is fairer, more realistic, or simply better than the listener's. Persuasion is how political minorities become majorities, creating the possibility of change and progress.[17] Persuasion depends on finding common values and mutual interests. To persuade someone to accept a particular view, one must link that view with other arguments, ideas, and information that can be shared by both parties. In a positive sense, political persuasion emphasizes common ground and ways to bridge differences between culture, values, and beliefs. Modern day participants in educational governance are more often limited to interpersonal influence and persuasion than organizational control. Control is associated with an outdated definition of governance and is no longer relevant due to the increasing complexity of public decision making.[18]

The use of language is a key feature of persuasion. Persuasive abilities include asking the right questions and determining when to be forceful or silent. When a topic is discussed in an individual's area of competency, a person can be forceful; and in areas where one is unsure or not knowledgeable, one must know when to remain silent yet attentive.

## Consensus Building and Collaboration

Many different terms can be used to describe the ability to work with groups to make decisions. Democratic approaches to governance require the skills of facilitation, collaboration, and consensus building. Effectiveness in group work is highly dependent on the qualities of the members and the nature of the decisions that must be made. Skillful facilitators use a combination of formal processes and interpersonal skills to confer, consult, and network among opposing or undecided group members. Prospective governance participants are urged to consider many of the methods and techniques in the growing field of conflict management and dispute resolution.

There is wide agreement that traditional organizational norms are being replaced by new cooperative norms that rely on the ability of small groups to make decisions. Governance participants work in partnership with teachers, parents, students, public and private agencies, and nonprofit organizations. As popular as collaborative decision making may be in the school improvement literature, it represents a dramatic shift from the traditional bureaucratic and hierarchical models of the past. Site-based management requires administrators and teachers to act as facilitators, not dictators. Many school leaders lack experience and knowledge about collaborative leadership and shared decision making with outside agencies.[19] Many preparation programs are beginning to define ways for prospective administrators to gain experience in consensus building and collaboration. Teachers and community members may have facilitation skills and experience in consensus building that administrators can draw upon. However, regardless of who serves as facilitator, site-based management depends upon all the members setting a collaborative tone and legitimately participating in a group decision-making process.

## Networking

Organizational research has demonstrated that a critical management skill is building and cultivating a network of friends and allies in order to obtain information and generate positive working relationships. Networks can be developed by knowing what people in the organization care about and framing an agenda to meet their needs. "The basic point is simple: as a manager, you need friends and allies to get things done."[20]

Formal networks in education refer to interagency partnerships and intergovernmental agreements. Educational administrators frequently deal with multiple networks, many outside the institutions they manage. Governance participants are finding that traditional approaches to school funding are not sufficient to meet community expectations for school reform. Partnerships designed to improve the historically weak links between schools and communities are being viewed as cost-saving mechanisms. School leaders are consequently involved with services and programs that are beyond their personal knowledge and expertise. Because human services are not administered directly by schools, an appreciation for the political dynamics of networks is required.

There are several important factors to consider in building partnerships between schools and external organizations. In the design of partnerships, school leaders may be accustomed to greater autonomy in articulating goals and setting priorities. The protocol and traditions of educators must be balanced with the managerial approaches of other members. Further, combining agency budgets, sustaining fiscal support, and sharing physical space can become problematic after partnerships are formed. The difficulty in sustaining interagency agreements reveals the degree to which administrators need to add networking skills to their list of required competencies.

## Conflict Management

Managing conflict can be viewed as synonymous with governing. In a fundamental sense, governance involves legal and authoritative approaches to controlling social behavior. Managing conflict is not the same as resolving conflicts between individuals and groups. Action-oriented administrators would like to resolve or eliminate conflicts. However, many organizational and personal conflicts may not be resolvable or avoidable. Conflicts generally do not come with clear causes and obvious components, but instead are obscured by the dynamics of organizational life. Conflict management is the ability to accept a reasonable degree of tension and uncertainty and to prevent it from escalating and interfering with important organizational goals.

Social and political forces in schools and educational systems inevitably generate conflict. A 1991 study reported that school administrators spend as much as 40 percent of their time in conflict management.[21] Preparation for conflict-filled environments includes an objective evaluation of a person's predisposition to conflict as well as a review of practical approaches to mediation, negotiation, and conflict management. There are many ways for groups to negotiate and come to agreements that require longer time frames and different approaches than authoritative efforts to *resolve* conflict. The field of conflict management and mediation has expanded in the last decade as an alternative to more costly legal avenues when dealing with disagreements. Figure 7.1 depicts a continuum of conflict management approaches.[22]

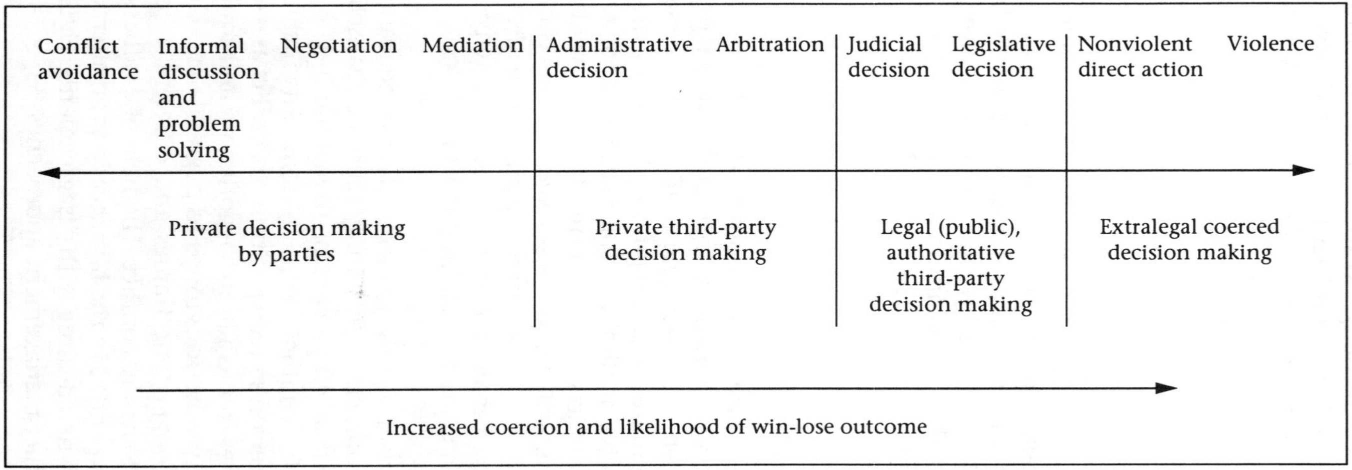

**FIGURE 7.1  Continuum of Conflict Management and Resolution Approaches**

Source: Moore, Christopher. "Approaches to Managing and Resolving Conflict." *The Mediation Process: Practical Strategies for Resolving Conflict*, p. 5. Copyright 1986 by Jossey-Bass, Inc., Publishers. Reprinted with permission.

This type of continuum can be helpful for governing boards in thinking openly about the costs of responding to conflicts and weighing them against the impact of the conflicts themselves. This diagram also helps identify the number of options available locally and the benefits of managing conflict at the level closest to where the problems emerge.

Mediation is the intervention into a dispute or negotiation by an acceptable and impartial third party. The mediator has no authoritative decision-making power to assist disputing parties in reaching their own settlement. Mediation extends informal bargaining into a new format that allows a mediator to contribute new variables and dynamics to the interaction. Principled bargaining separates the people from the problem and focuses on identifying common interests instead of rigid positions.[23] Negotiation is composed of a series of complex activities or "moves" differing parties initiate to resolve differences and manage conflicts.

## ETHICAL LEADERSHIP

Leadership abilities are essential in political settings. Just as governors are generally considered leaders, participants in governance are expected to provide leadership. A skillful leader is seen as someone who is able to get people to get things done. Leadership requires a mix of interpersonal skills, knowledge, and the elusive qualities of intuition, inspiration, and vision.

Although the call for leaders is widespread, leadership as an activity is an enigma. There is no shortage of images of school leadership emerging from the literature in education, or consensus among academics and practitioners on what constitutes ideal school leadership.[24] Many ideas about leadership follow the popular phrase that distinguishes between managers who "do the thing right," and leaders who "do the right thing." However, managing and leading are interrelated responsibilities, and for practical purposes both skills should be considered necessary and important.

Leadership is particularly enigmatic in the context of democratic governance. Participation in governance inevitably means group work and achieving consensus in a community or in an organization that serves a community. Democratic governance is an activity that requires the efforts of many citizens, not just individuals who, by virtue of their elected office, expertise, or position, have the ability to influence or the legal authority to control decision making.[25] The more widespread the ability and willingness to take initiative and to consider others' initiatives, the more effective the community will be and the less pressure there will be on particular individuals to take on the role of leader.

History too often focuses narrowly on visible leaders and presents the wrong impression about leadership processes. The skills of leaders are deduced from the traits among legendary and mythical individuals. Leaders are depicted as dramatic figures associated with radical individualism and the movies. What gets left out of these images are the dangers of centralizing authority and dominating the followers. The separation of powers in American government was designed specifically to prevent the accumulation of power by positional leaders, particularly in the executive branch.

Democratic principles suggest that public schools will be better served by broad-based leadership than the efforts of individuals. Leadership *in* a school, instead of leadership *of* a school, is both an end and a means.[26] Few would disagree that the challenges in public education are serious enough to require the involvement of communities of leaders. Community leadership does not downplay the important roles of those formally charged with being *leaders*. It suggests both top-down and bottom-up leadership are needed simultaneously.

In order to avoid the overly-individualized, ego-driven side of leadership and authority, leadership can be considered as a subset of other kinds of important actions and a measure of authentic involvement.[27] Leadership skills in educational governance have as much to do with patience and maturity as transformation and visioning. Community leadership requires the ability to sit through long public meetings and honestly listen to those with opposing views. It often means showing up and participating in community events and being helpful to people at odd hours. Flexibility and openness are critical in order to accept and then improve upon the dynamic nature of democratic governance.

The close connection between governance and politics requires educational leaders to think carefully about the ethical implications of their decisions. Aristotle argued long ago that "it is not enough to know about goodness and ethical conduct, men must pursue goodness in society and practice goodness in politics."[28] Educational governance represents an important opportunity to promote and demonstrate ethical behavior. Because of the moral and political dimensions of teaching and learning, educational governance has powerful ethical overtones. If politics is about power, ethics is about where and how power is directed.

For elected and nonelected governance participants who genuinely wish to do the right thing, there are many ways to think about ethics.[29] Codes of conduct and formal rules are only one source of ethical direction. These documents can be useful, but they tend to offer broad and idealistic visions or prescriptive ways of avoiding evil. They are of limited value to school administrators facing the immediacy of conflicts and the need to make important public decisions.

Another approach to ethics takes the form of agency ethics—doing what's best for the organization rather than the community at large.

Organizational cultures often enforce ethics that avoid embarrassing the agency, even at the expense of withholding significant truths from the public. When public schools and educators are routinely criticized, it is not surprising when many administrators substitute their personal beliefs for public ethics. Educational leaders describe their ethics as founded on common sense and personal values. However, experience demonstrates that common sense tends to be neither common nor always sensible.

What practitioners need is a way of thinking about secular ethics that can guide them in attempting to "do the right thing" in the context of American democratic values. A precondition for ethical behavior is the understanding that the exercise of public power is tantamount to governing. Public ethics implies adherence to the values of those who are governed. Public values are built into the concept of the "common good" which is codified in the laws of the land. Not only are public values embedded in the law, they are the operating principles for educational leaders.

In searching for ways of thinking about ethics, participants in governance must first look to the highest level of law for guidance. The U.S. Constitution and the constitutions of the fifty states are good starting points for ethical inquiry. The Bill of Rights, in particular, offers sound and practical guidance. U.S. Supreme Court cases and opinions offer another useful source of ethical insight in our democracy.

Diversity within communities and school systems creates situations in which the personal ethics of administrators and policy makers clash with other members of a governance group. To the extent one can identify the ethical values of the community, Hirschman summarizes three basic ethical choices: exit, voice and loyalty.[30]

1. One can act with *loyalty* in accordance with the community's ethics;
2. One can exercise First Amendment freedoms to challenge community ethics (*voice*), both within the public institution as an educator and, in most cases, publicly as a private citizen, but;
3. When personal ethics make it impossible to act loyally in one's official capacity and voicing objection becomes counterproductive, resignation (*exit*) is the only ethical option.

The popular cliché referring to a critical ethical skill is "picking your battles." Voicing ethical concerns or eventually resigning is a tough standard, but one befitting the special trust granted to public educators in the context of democracy. Resignation of competent and ethically motivated educational leaders over matters of little consequence is not advised. Acting contrary to the ethical values of the community is a serious issue, for it strikes at the most basic principles of American democracy. Consequently, being ethical in educational governance requires a careful understanding of community values and an informed sense of the common good.

## ORGANIZING AND BALANCING SKILL REQUIREMENTS

Comprehensive lists of knowledge and skill requirements require administrators (and their preparation programs) to cover traditional domains of knowledge while adding new skill requirements associated with the increasing complexity of public school systems. The limits of what administrators are supposed to know about *educating* as well as managing and governing are unclear. The National Association of Elementary School Principals, for example, produced a list of seventy-four proficiencies grouped into ten categories to define the expert principal.[31]

Aspiring administrators need creative ways to organize knowledge and skill requirements into a manageable form. Research in several fields has demonstrated that symbols and metaphors can be used as methods for organizing knowledge and understanding organizations. Metaphors exert a formative influence on our language and how we think: "By using different metaphors to understand the complex and paradoxical character of organizational life, we are able to manage and design organizations in ways that we may not have thought possible before."[32]

In order to make sense out of a massive amount of information, two broad metaphors can be used to organize critical governance skills—the manager/economist and the colleague/communitarian. There are strong traditions supporting both of these metaphors for educational leadership. The manager/economist image is similar to a rational-bureaucratic conceptualization of schools, while the colleague/communitarian approach to governance is comparable to the personnel-communal image.[33]

### Manager/Economist

The manager/economist uses rational, economic arguments to make decisions based on professional training and technical expertise. The key values driving this approach are efficiency and effectiveness. The principles of outcome-based education are phrased within the language of the sciences and private sector models of production and quality assurance.

The manager/economist is consequently adept at discussing educational reforms with representatives from the business community. He or she provides specific ideas and explanations for human motivation, organizational behavior, and politics from the economic principles of self-interest and market-based competition. The manager/economist approach has been popular in educational administration for a long time, just as the scientific method of inquiry has flourished in the social sciences. Many believe economic thinking is the dominant paradigm in American culture, politics, and educational policy.[34]

## Colleague/Communitarian

The colleague/communitarian participant in governance works to create a sense of community in a school through communication and collegiality. As an administrator, she or he supports cooperative efforts among members of the school culture by removing structural and bureaucratic barriers that prevent integrated approaches to teaching and learning. Education is viewed as a collective process designed to achieve social justice, equality, and open communication.

The colleague/communitarian seeks the knowledge base and skills associated with the human relations school of management and organizational culture. Applying the communitarian approach requires careful consideration of the degree to which the larger educational establishment (school districts, state boards of education, and national organizations) supports communitarian values of truth, equity, and social justice. Communitarians argue that schools must first and foremost nurture democratic values. They believe that cultures of excellence can also support economic interests.[35]

Economic and cultural metaphors for school leadership are not mutually exclusive or completely incompatible. Both of these images are important when they are applied to an institution as complex and multifaceted as public education. There are times when one value frame is more important or relevant to an administrative problem than the other. For example, components of school budgeting and finance lend themselves to businesslike approaches. Teaching and learning, on the other hand, are enhanced by a sense of community. The challenge for administrators and members of governance committees is to promote a comprehensive understanding of schools that draw from both metaphors.

## SUMMARY

Effective participation in governance requires a combination of factual knowledge and interpersonal skills. Governance skills are indirectly defined as subsets of professional competencies for principals, superintendents, and teachers. This chapter emphasizes the kinds of competencies that encourage broad participation in governance.

The technical knowledge relevant to educational governance is generally viewed as part of the knowledge base of educational administration. The technology of education refers to the many theories and methods that explain how students learn and how teachers teach. Descriptions of educational administration as a profession and a field of knowledge include virtually all the traditional areas of knowledge associated with management in the private sector and in public agencies.

Governance skills can be viewed as applied political knowledge. Competence in governance is largely a function of understanding how to operate in a social and political environment. Becoming effective in governance requires some explicit knowledge about public policies as well as experience in public decision making. Reflection, intuition, and thoughtfulness are the kinds of skills needed for anyone who is entering the political and value-laden arena of educational governance.

Politics is the art and science of using influence, authority, and power to achieve important goals. Political skills, like technical skills, are tools for getting things done. Political competence requires knowledge and skill in building a power base, persuasion, consensus building and collaboration, networking, and conflict management.

Skills associated with organizational communications include the ability to formulate and implement policies related to the exchange of information. School and system-wide policies range from media relations to managing electronic communication systems to the curricular implications of instructional technology. Technological change in the workplace and the dynamic quality of the information age underscore the importance of information and computer literacy as requisite communication skill.

Leadership abilities are essential in complex political settings. The close connection between governance and politics requires educational leaders to think carefully about the ethical implications of their decisions. While there are many ways to think about ethics, public ethics implies adherence to the values of those who are governed. Being ethical in educational governance requires a careful understanding of community values and an informed sense of the common good.

In order to make sense out of a massive amount of information, two broad metaphors can be used to organize critical governance skills—the manager/economist and the colleague/communitarian. The challenge for administrators is to develop an approach to school leadership that draws from both metaphors.

## SEMINAR QUESTIONS

1. If you were to prioritize the three most important skills for effective participation in governance, what would they be?

2. How can educational policy makers improve the image of politics in education?

3. What is your personal philosophy of educational leadership?

4. If you were to design a graduate program in educational administration, what would be the design and sequence of coursework and learning experiences?

## SUGGESTED READINGS

Fisher, Roger and William Ury. *Getting to Yes.* New York: Houghton-Mifflin, 1981.

*The Kettering Review* (Dayton, Ohio: Kettering Foundation). This quarterly journal includes a wide array of contributors who share ideas about "the changing role of the citizen, the press, and public leadership, and the role of public deliberation in our complex modern democracy."

Moore, Christopher W. *The Mediation Process: Practice Strategies for Resolving Conflict.* San Francisco: Jossey-Bass, 1986.

Schon, Donald. *The Reflective Practitioner.* New York: Basic Books, 1983.

Sergiovanni, Thomas. *The Principalship: A Reflective Practice Perspective.* Needham Heights, Mass.: Allyn & Bacon, 1991.

## ENDNOTES

1. Thomas J. Sergiovanni, *The Principalship: A Reflective Practice Perspective* (Needham Heights, Mass.: Allyn & Bacon, 1991), p. 5.

2. Carl D. Glickman "Pushing School Reform to a New Edge: The Seven Ironies of School Empowerment," *Phi Delta Kappan* (September 1990), p. 63.

3. James M. Smith, "Examining Praxis: Espying From the University and the School Site," *Journal of School Leadership*, vol. 4, no. 1 (January 1994), p. 9.

4. Thelbert L. Drake and William H. Roe, *School Business Management* (Boston: Allyn & Bacon, 1994). Also see Roald F. Campbell, et al., *The Organization and Control of American Schools* (Columbus, Ohio: Merrill Publishing, 1980).

5. *Principals for Our Changing Schools,* ed. Scott D. Thomson (Fairfax, Va.: National Policy Board for Educational Administration, 1993).

6. William Foster, "A Critical Perspective on Administration and Organization in Education," in *Critical Perspectives on the Organization and Improvement of Schooling,* eds. Kenneth A. Sirotnik and Jeannie Oakes (Boston: Kluver-Nijhoff Publishing, 1986).

7. Sergiovanni, *The Principalship: A Reflective Practice Perspective,* p. 18.

8. Rosabeth M. Kanter, *The Change Masters* (New York: Simon & Schuster, 1983).

9. Peter Block, *The Empowered Manager* (San Francisco: Jossey-Bass, 1991).

10. Larry W. Hughes, *The Principal as Leader* (New York: Macmillan Publishing, 1994). Also see Edward A. Duane, William M. Bridgeland, and Michael E. Stern, "The Leadership of Principals: Coping with Turbulence," *Education,* vol. 107, no. 2 (1992) pp. 212–219.

11. Lee G. Bolman and Terrence E. Deal, *Reframing Organizations* (San Francisco: Jossey-Bass, 1991).
12. Rodney Muth, Michael J. Murphy and W. Michael Martin "Problem-Based Learning at the University of Colorado at Denver," *Journal of School Leadership*, vol. 4 (1994), p. 432.
13. Michael Usdan, "Emerging Leadership Needs in Education," *National Civic Review*, vol. 80, no. 1 (Winter 1991), p. 49.
14. Ernesto Cortes Jr., *Kettering Review* (Dayton, Ohio: Kettering Foundation, Summer 1993), p. 34.
15. Wilma A. Smith and Richard L. Andrews, *Instructional Leadership: How Principals Make a Difference* (Alexandria, Va.: Association for Supervision and Curriculum Development, 1989).
16. Karen F. Osterman, "Communication Skills: A Key to Collaboration and Change," *Journal of School Leadership*, vol. 4, no. 4 (July 1994), p. 386.
17. Guy Molyneux, "Political Debate: Americans Today Just Don't Get It," *The Los Angeles Times* (May 23, 1994).
18. Cora Marrett, "School Organization and the Quest for Community," *Choice and Control in American Education*, vol. 1, ed. William H. Clune and John F. Witte (New York: Falmer Press, 1990), p. 237.
19. Jeanne Jehl and Michael Kirst, "Getting Ready to Provide School-Linked Services: What Schools Must Do," in *The Future of Children*, vol. 2, no. 1 (Center for the Future of Children, Spring 1992).
20. Bolman and Deal, *Reframing Organizations*, p. 211.
21. Charles T. Araki, "Managing Conflict in the Schools with System 4," *National Forum of Educational Administration and Supervision Journal* vol. 7, no. 2 (1990), pp. 18–30.
22. Christopher W. Moore, *The Mediation Process* (San Francisco: Jossey-Bass, 1986), p. 5.
23. Roger Fisher and William Ury, *Getting to Yes* (New York: Houghton-Mifflin, 1981).
24. Kenneth A. Leighwood, Paul T. Begley, and J. Bradly Cousins, *Developing Expert Leadership for Future Schools* (London: Falmer Press, 1992).
25. Michael Briand, "People, Lead Thyself," *Kettering Review* (Dayton, Ohio: Kettering Foundation, Summer 1993), pp. 38–46.
26. Joseph T. Murphy "The Unheroic Side of Leadership: Notes from the Swamp," *Phi Delta Kappan*, vol. 68, no. 9 (May 1988), pp. 654–659.
27. Robert W. Terry, *Authentic Leadership* (San Francisco: Jossey-Bass, 1993).
28. Mortimer J. Adler, *Reforming Education* (New York: Macmillan Publishing, 1988).
29. Kenneth H. Torp, "Ethics For Public Administrators," *National Civic Review*, vol. 83, no. 1 (Denver: National Civic League, Winter-Spring 1994), pp. 70–73.
30. Albert Hirshman, *Exit, Voice and Loyalty: Responses to Decline in Firms, Organizations and States* (Cambridge, Mass.: Harvard University Press, 1970).
31. *Elementary and Middle School Proficiencies for Principals* (Alexandria, Va.: National Association of Elementary School Principals, 1986).

32. Gareth Morgan, *Images of Organization* (Newbury Park, California: Sage Publications, 1986), p. 13.

33. Anthony S. Bryk, Valerie E. Lee and Julia B. Smith, "High School Organization and Its Effects on Teachers and Students: An Interpretive Summary of the Research," in *Choice and Control in American Education*, vol. 1, ed. William H. Clune and John F. Witte (New York: Falmer Press, 1990) pp. 135–226.

34. David P. Ericson, "On Critical Theory and Educational Practice," in *Critical Perspectives on the Organization and Improvement of Schooling*, eds. Kenneth A. Sirotnik and Jeannie Oakes (Boston: Kluver-Nijhoff Publishing, 1986). Also see William L. Boyd, "The Power of Paradigms: Reconceptualizing Educational Policy and Management," *Educational Administration Quarterly*, vol. 28, no. 4 (November 1992), p. 504.

35. William C. Cummingham and Donn W. Gresso, *Cultural Leadership* (Needham Heights, Mass.: Allyn & Bacon, 1993). Also see Ann Lieberman, *Schools as Collaborative Cultures: Creating the Future Now* (New York: Falmer Press, 1990).

# 8

# THE FUTURE OF
# EDUCATIONAL GOVERNANCE

*The act of governing can never
be without consequences.*
—Danzberger, Kirst, and Usdan
in *Governing Public Schools*

From informal discussions in the homes of concerned parents to debates between candidates for national office, educational policy makers are contemplating major changes in the way schools are governed. After decades and waves of school reform with questionable impacts, there is growing interest in moving the sponsorship of schools from district-based governance systems to a variety of privatized models of school control.

The four sectors involved in educational decisions will continue to influence the policy process through the values and traditions of the institutions they represent. The public sector, represented by the current system of federal, state, and local education agencies, includes complex and paradoxical movements to establish national goals and site-based decision making. The private sector, represented by economic interests and the market orientation of business and industry, continues to advocate for greater competition, consumer choice, and the privatization of public education. The nonprofit sector and the media appear to be gaining greater influence in the governing process without representing a consistent set of reform-related values.

Many of the issues facing the four sectors of governance in the coming years are identified in this chapter. Improvements in the current system of public governance and the implications of moving to a private system are discussed in light of the traditional purposes of public education. Throughout this chapter, recommendations for the future of educational governance are offered to promote a balance among social and political values supporting American education.

## CHALLENGES TO THE PUBLIC SECTOR AND DEMOCRATIC GOVERNANCE

Within the current system of district-based governance, formal policies are the result of public decisions made by democratically elected policy makers. There are inefficiencies inherent in a system of multiple layers of governmental responsibility and political authority. At the local level, lack of participation in school board elections undermines the degree to which the school district system is truly democratic. If only 10 percent of eligible voters participate in a school election, a small percentage of a potentially un-representative group can control the formation of community-wide policies.

There are serious challenges to state-level governance structures related to raising and equitably allocating revenues for public education. A 1994 Gallop Poll reported that people generally believe the existing U.S. system of tax funding for public schools is unfair to the average citizen.[1] A majority of state governments are also dealing with legal challenges to school finance systems. Many people believe that the whole functioning of education governance, from the federal to the local level, needs to be assessed, expectations need to be redefined, and current structural and behavioral barriers to participation need to be lowered.

### Balancing Political Authority

Historically, governance reforms have emphasized shifts in political authority between federal, state, and local levels of government. Current reforms can be classified according to their underlying emphasis on centralizing or decentralizing decision making. Achieving a balance between the forces of centralized government and local control will continue to be a complicated issue as well as an opportunity for reform within the existing system of public governance.

Local control of schools is a hallmark of Jeffersonian democracy and a structural expression of American's distrust of big government. Decentralizing governance is the direct effect of site-based management, teacher empowerment models, and designation of school sites as the centers of change. Research in the 1980s demonstrated the ineffectiveness of policies that leave out teachers and classroom-level considerations. Advocates of decentralization argue that many of the factors associated with academically effective education are school and neighborhood based, even though control and financing have shifted to state and national institutions. Sirotnik states: "If schools and what goes on inside them are not at the center of the educational ecology, then current efforts toward change and improvement are horribly misguided."[2]

The proponents of centralizing governance authority represent a powerful coalition of political and economic interests. The excellence movement includes public and private sector leaders who advocate centralizing the state's control of schools through curricular mandates and standardized testing programs. State legislatures and state education agencies attempt to control and monitor classroom inputs, processes, and outcomes. Advocates of more centralized authority include both Republican and Democratic presidents, members of Congress, and a majority of the nation's governors who prescribe national standards and goals for all of America's schools. Representatives of national organizations point to the success of school systems in Europe that mandate national standards through centralized educational policies. The argument is made that world class standards can not be left to the whimsy of 15,000 local communities or individual schools. Susan Tift, an associate editor of *Time* magazine, exemplifies the fervor behind the movement to a more centralized system: "It is critical that the country face up to the myth of state and local control and begin to implement a national education system with thought and consciousness, preserving what works and opening to experimentation the many areas that need overhauling."[3]

Arguments for centralizing and decentralizing governance have continued for decades, resulting in a variety of political compromises in the fifty states. In many cases, power shifts have resulted in more complex and inefficient structures for schooling and governance. The long-term consequence of intergovernmentalism is a system with so many levels of government that all are nominally responsible for education, yet none are truly responsible.[4] The complexity of intergovernmentalism is particularly challenging for school principals operating in a precarious middle ground between the demands of their school communities and the mandates of school districts, state agencies, and federal program guidelines. Overlapping governance demands on school principals create a sense of uncertainty and contradiction.

The combined effects of decentralization and centralization will challenge the utility and authority of the school district system, and to a lesser degree, the role of the states in educational policy. School districts operate between the forces of school-based governance and centralized authority. The district system is consequently where many of the battles over political control will occur.

State governments face a different set of political problems. The current emphasis on site-based management is to a large degree a rejection of state-based reforms, criticized as insensitive to local-level educators. State governments are also facing political challenges in the form of ballot initiatives, referendums, and constitutional amendments that bypass the authority of state legislatures and state agencies. Figure 8.1 displays the different levels of governance and the forces of intergovernmentalism on school districts and state education agencies.

Large urban districts are at the center of controversy and pressure toward change. Educating the majority of American students, urban districts are facing serious organizational problems above and beyond the decline of inter-city neighborhoods and decreasing financial support. Bureaucratic districts are struggling with coordination costs among departments and schools. Communication problems prevent governing boards and central administrators from getting full information from administrators and teachers. These issues are quickly eroding public support for public education. Taxpayers are becoming distrustful of educators who appear to be fighting over the power to reform instead of conducting reform. William Boyd's use of the terms *schizophrenia* and *paranoia* aptly identify the increasing problem of political confusion and intergovernmental uncertainty.[5]

Intergovernmental issues and political turf battles have stifled reform in the public sector for decades. Reforms in education, based on integrated human services in schools, are a powerful example of the contradictions policy makers are facing. On one hand, administrators are expected to increase efficiency through better coordination of services with other public agencies. While school-based partnerships between public and private organizations have proven to be effective ways to maximize services to students and families, the involvement of multiple

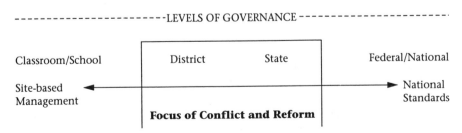

FIGURE 8.1   **Intergovernmental Issues**

organizations in decision making creates confusion and intergovernmental coordination costs. Parent groups are often divided over the issue
of providing human services in schools, and educational leaders are left
with no clear direction or mandate for change.

American school systems need policies that reflect a practical balance between intergovernmental authority and the interests of centralization and decentralization. More experienced policy makers are trying
to decide which components of governance are best handled at different
levels of authority; and regardless of the specific outcomes of these negotiations, wise administrators appreciate the importance of developing
skills in intergovernmental management and collaborative approaches
to decision making.

## REBUILDING DEMOCRACY
## IN THE PUBLIC SYSTEM

In order to make lasting improvements in public governance, changes
must go beyond the system's structure. Changes must focus on deeper
cultural values and mind-sets that affect behavior. The central question
in governance reform is interpreting the meaning of the word *public* in
public education. The public purposes of schooling require a democratic
system of decision making, both as a means of school control and a
demonstration of political values. Beyond benefiting the individual, the
primary purpose of the American system of free schools is to prepare
young people to maintain and strengthen a democratic society. The public schools are the best place to start rebuilding American democracy.

There are many ways for schools to incorporate more democratic
and participatory approaches to decision making. Public systems of governance are also open to authoritarian approaches to administration and
control, particularly when community participation is limited. Public
agencies are vulnerable to bureaucratic pathologies which complicate
efforts to promote democratic values and inclusive governance dialogues. However, bureaucracies can be redesigned to provide organizational stability and individual creativity. Innovations in both public and
private sector organizations are available for educational leaders committed to improving the public schools.

National organizations and school-based management groups are
actively promoting new ways to involve the community in school decision making. The Institute for Educational Leadership, for example, rec-
ommends that school board elections be held along with general elections to increase voter awareness and community-wide participation.[6]

Reforms must also be directed at the informal aspects of governance. The protocol of school board meetings and the nature of school-community relations have a direct impact on the quality of governance. Administrators and policy makers can create settings that provide a greater sense of unity and meaningful exchange. What is needed is a form of participatory democracy in which citizens become capable of expressing a common purpose by virtue of positive civic attitudes and participatory institutions.[7] The popularity of site-based management is an indication of the interest in rebuilding democratic values in public schools. Educators are also looking at some of the ways other public agencies are increasing citizen involvement and facilitating greater participation. The fundamental issue in reform is attitudinal—whether Americans believe public institutions can function effectively to prepare students for democratic citizenship.

## Reframing the Politics of Education

Politics is an inevitable aspect of any public system or democratic forum. School leaders must accept and even welcome the political side of public organizations; but gaining political skills requires a constructive and positive definition of politics. Politics can be defined in relation to citizenship, conflict management, and collective action to benefit the interests of the community. Governance participants can begin to support political debates that focus on broader issues and core American values without feeling like politics is inherently unethical.

The traditional belief in political neutrality in education, combined with widespread cynicism about government and politics, has suppressed the quality and character of many governance dialogues. Opinion polls and conversations with administrators continue to show how negative definitions of politics curtail community involvement in public forums. However, governance and politics will go on, even when participation is minimal. If politics is redefined as something essential and practical, citizens might return to political settings. Politically active communities may be more contentious, but they are less likely to respond to narrow interests and authoritarian management styles.

As people become involved in governance, policy makers and administrators need to frame issues in ways that acknowledge the delicate balance of community values and the trade-offs of school reform. Many people will be searching for technical solutions to problems, even though value conflicts are not problems to be solved by scientific methods. They are dilemmas that require political negotiation and compromises among policy makers and interest groups. Educational politics are much like the hard political problems that occur in other public institutions. There are no easy solutions, there are only political trade-offs.[8] Effective participation in governance through site-based management requires the ability to stay engaged in debates that are marked by conflict and compromise. If public school systems become more open to politics, the tenor of school-community relations can evolve from defensive public relations campaigns to more honest approaches that invite community participation in the process of change.

## PRIVATIZING PUBLIC EDUCATION

The public educational system seems to be too large and entrenched to ever be seriously challenged by private approaches to schooling. However, a combination of political and social forces in the 1990s could bring about significant change. First, dissatisfaction with public schools and distrust of public institutions show no signs of diminishing. Movements to limit taxes through local and state-wide initiatives, voter referendums, and constitutional amendments are increasing, both in number and degree of impact on local school districts. Anti-government sentiment in the 1990s is associated with a shift to more conservative social and political values. Observers have described the combined effects of these forces as the privatization of American life, emphasizing a reduced role for government, greater parental control, and an emphasis on efficiency and individuality.

Greater interest in private approaches to public issues follows years of costly and ineffective school reforms. Many of the efforts promoting excellence in the 1980s were founded on criticisms of noncompetitive, monopolistic public schools. Observing a new wave of reform, William Boyd warned in 1987: "Suppose then, that the excellence movement falters, public school performance lags, and there is growing acceptance of research claiming to document the inefficiency of public schools as compared to private schools. . . . If this happens, we then could witness the political sea change necessary for the creation of a new balance between public and private schools."[9] A political shift is apparently taking place as more private organizations are being asked to manage public school systems and new versions of market-based reforms emerge. In 1993, the best-seller *Reinventing Government* proclaimed: "In today's fast-moving marketplace, the private sector is rapidly taking market share away from public organizations. Public schools are losing ground to private schools."[10] The continuing privatization of American life, combined with the influence and popularity of the private sector in educational governance are likely to sustain pressures for market-based schools of choice.

Private approaches to governance are fundamentally different from public decision making systems. Governance through private choice includes voucher systems, schools of choice, and reforms associated with privatizing different components of the public system. Private systems of governance are dictated by the decisions of families as consumers of educational services. The principles of market-based competition work to "govern" the quality and character of schools.

Privatization is closely aligned with the involvement of the business community in school reform. Privatization is founded on the basic theories of economics. Principles of self interest and the supply and demand of scarce resources are used as guides to understanding and organizing human affairs. Advocates believe in requiring public schools to compete with private schools and freeing up market forces to drive bad schools out of business. The market analogy is employed as a root metaphor for explaining events and recommending solutions. The arguments that follow hold that financial support for education should be allocated as a direct benefit to children rather than to institutions. Current versions of vouchers and tuition tax credits would extend support to families to pay tuition to an expanding market of private schools and privatized public schools.

Business-oriented approaches to governance are reflected in initiatives to make the purposes of commerce foremost in the goals of public education and to model the private sector's orientation and methods in operating schools. Critics have argued that *A Nation at Risk* was a prime example of making the economy's needs paramount in judging and reforming education.[11] Others point out that governance changes based on Total Quality Management are new versions of the factory model of schooling with a primary emphasis on organizational efficiency and economic prosperity.

## Opportunities and Issues

The advantages of privatized models of governance for schools are consistent with the benefits of competition and market economics. Greater competition in education will in all likelihood keep costs down and force public schools to respond more closely to the needs of their customers. Free markets reward innovation and boost the morale of workers as shareholders.[12] Because they will be new, privatized schools present the opportunity to implement a comprehensive package of innovations, including curricular, instructional, organizational, and governance changes in one program. Families choosing schools based on similar values can build a sense of community out of their commonality.

The benefits of private models must also be weighed against potential liabilities. Choice arrangements are likely to intensify a school's orientation to the private benefits of individuals over the public purposes of education. There are serious concerns about equal opportunity and access to privatized schools. Choice advocates need to consider how to avoid intensifying ethnic and socioeconomic segregation in the schools that are chosen. Research has demonstrated strong correlations between the selection of schools and child-rearing tendencies.[13] Middle-class and affluent parents often select more innovative schools for their youngsters, while working-class parents gravitate toward back-to-basics and fundamental schools. Care must be taken to avoid themes for privatized schools that could increase racial and socioeconomic isolation that is already occurring in many urban areas.

A related issue is the advertising and marketing of privatized schools. Some families will be more active shoppers for good schools. Inactive consumers who are not apprised of the implications of their choices may not choose a school that suits their needs and interests. The families most prone to take advantage of the choice option are the more educated and informed. Jonothon Kozol questions many of the positive assumptions about market forces in education, whether they are applied to public or private school systems:

> School boards think that if they offer the same printed information to all parents, they have made choice equally accessible. That is not true, of course, because the printed information won't be read, or certainly will not be scrutinized aggressively, by parents who can't read or who read very poorly. . . . The (Bush) White House, in advancing the agenda for a "choice" plan, rests its faith on market mechanisms. What reason have the black and very poor to lend their credence to a market system that has proved so obdurate and so resistant to their pleas at every turn? Placing the burden on the individual to break down doors in finding better education for a child is attractive to conservatives because it reaffirms their faith in individual ambition and autonomy. But to ask an individual to break down doors that have been chained and bolted in advance of his arrival is unfair.[14]

Both proponents and opponents of choice systems and privatization recognize that the interests of less-informed and low-income families will need protecting. One of the risks in any competitive approach to schooling is the costs of failure. In the economic marketplace, business failure equates to bankruptcy and a loss of money for shareholders. The failure of a noncompetitive school has serious consequences for human beings, who cannot be reimbursed for the most formative years of their lives.

## THE EXPANDING INFLUENCE OF THE NONPROFIT SECTOR AND THE MEDIA

Recent developments in public education are increasing the involvement and authority of the nonprofit sector. The charter schools concept allows nonprofit organizations, including human service agencies and universities, to operate schools and receive school finance dollars previously allocated to school districts. The popularity of integrated services and partnerships between schools and human service agencies increases the governance role of nonprofit organizations.

Whether the American education system retains and improves its current governance system or converts to privatized models, nonprofit organizations and the media will continue to play a major role in decision making. Organizations operating outside and in between the public and private sectors are powerful and entrenched institutions. Continued uncertainty within the public system works to the advantage of pressure groups with sophisticated political strategies designed to influence public policies. Political pluralism at the national level empowers special interests to lobby for and against education-related reforms. At the state and local levels of governance, nonprofit organizations continue to be well funded and highly effective.

The availability of reliable information about schools underscores the importance of the media in the functions of governance. Legislators, school boards, parents, and taxpayers rely heavily on the media to guide their decisions. Individuals who control the flow of information and opinion about education are increasingly influential in the policy process. Some of the most powerful educational positions in the United States are education editors and reporters.[15]

The media will have an expanded role in privatized models of schooling. Educators need the print media, radio, and television to recruit students and communicate their mission, methods, and offerings. If the marketing principles of the private sector translate to schools of choice, competition will require greater expertise and expense in the business of advertising and promotion. The burden of proof of a school's quality in a market-based educational system will derive from media-generated information to provide parents and taxpayers the ability to monitor, evaluate, and improve schools.

The growth of the knowledge industry and mass communications includes many other ways for the media to shape educational policies.[16] Policy makers will face a growing list of technical, regulatory, and curricular issues as the use of instructional technology increases. The effects of the media on representative democracy need to be examined in relation to the electoral process and school board reform. Media campaigns for elected office are often more about selling personalities than rational discussions of issues or formal approaches to public accountability. Despite the quality of reporting, the power of the media will continue to influence public opinion about the quality of schools.

## SYSTEM-WIDE CONCERNS AND RECOMMENDATIONS

Significant changes in governance represent shifts in political power and are consequently loaded with opportunities and issues. School districts and states are experimenting with market-oriented modifications of governance with mixed results. Major reforms designed to improve the current system of public governance and rebuild the citizenry's confidence in public education are ongoing. Yet every so-called solution to a governance problem presents contradictions and trade-offs. Both public and private approaches to education and governance generate so many secondary questions that simple solutions are no longer available.

Americans are at a point in history where improvements in governance must incorporate a greater diversity of cultures and beliefs than that which exists in any other country. As one retired administrator warned, "This isn't Norway, we better figure out a system that deals with our diversity, and it won't be easy!" Advocates of fundamental changes need to take into account the resiliency and effectiveness of current forms of governance. The American political system has demonstrated the capacity to forge a single nation from peoples of diverse racial, religious, and ethnic origins. We cannot succeed with a nation based on separate ethnic communities and non-negotiable rights of pressure groups. Americans must prevent differences from escalating into antagonism and hatred.[17] The inadequacy of past reforms has demonstrated that real changes in schools will require the input and cooperation of educators within the system as well as the involvement of policy makers and community members from outside the schools. Continuing divisions and distrust between educators and community members pose the most serious threat to school improvement.

### *Balancing American Values in Education*

The choice between a public or a private educational system is a major statement of American values. If the present system of governance through local school districts is retained, there is little doubt that reform will need to occur. However, retaining and improving the current structure will signal an investment in the public schools, the nation's only tax supported institutions that have as their main purpose the education of students to become citizens of a democratic society.[18] If private systems of education continue to expand and diversify, Americans will be making a different statement of values. Privatizing public education places a priority on individual benefits and a more competitive orientation to schooling.

Choosing between a public or private educational system will neither be simple nor definitive. The size, scope, and decentralized qualities of public education will require a series of state and local policy changes before a predominantly privatized system can emerge. The details involved in implementing a governance change of this magnitude could overshadow the underlying shift in beliefs and values about education. Policy makers need to consider whether a majority of Americans are willing to make fundamental changes in the balance of public and private purposes of education.

Chapter 5 identified five political values in educational governance: liberty, equality, efficiency, economic development, and community. Governance reforms in the 1990s appear to favor the values of liberty (in the form of school choice) and efficiency (privatization) over other political values. Efficiency gains in the governing process need to be weighed against potential losses in opportunities for open and equal participation. Recent studies of state policy making describe a consistent pattern in the pursuit of four political values; from quality to efficiency to equity, with choice remaining as a priority throughout.[19] The value of community is missing from these priorities and is rarely discussed in the formal context of educational governance. Learning communities are consistently acknowledged as valuable in a pedagogical sense; but the importance of building community as a social and political value appears to be losing ground in the pursuit of efficiency and choice.

Common belief systems are at least as important as formal patterns of governance in shaping American education.[20] Participants in governance must therefore recognize the importance of setting priorities among competing values. As the nation's largest expenditure of public funds outside of the military, educational policies will have a sizable impact on schools. They can also help rebuild communities in the 21st Century.

## *Strengthening the Value of Community*

Changes in governance need to consider education's public purposes and the importance of creating a sense of community. Educators are not alone in recognizing the breakdown of community life and the decline of public values. It seems that the intensity of debates over "family values" and "political correctness" has polarized and divided many Americans from a sense of community. Challenges to public life have become as serious as crime and violence and as politically sensitive as immigration and suburbanization. The sociologist Robert Bellah summarizes the problem of community in America as the consequence of a trend toward "private affluence and public squalor."[21]

Historically, public education has played a key role in community building. As institutions, local schools are the gathering place for families and the meeting ground for public forums. As learning environments, schools have served as the source of knowledge about American culture and core political values. Recent reforms appear to be aimed more at economic interests and international competitiveness. As important as these goals are, they may not be responsive to the problems of community building. When the prime motivation for educational excellence is economic prosperity the educational process can diminish rather than foster community. Competition in schools can make one child's success dependent on another's failure. This kind of competition weakens the social bond because it teaches students to attend to personal interests rather than social needs.[22]

School systems are central to the relationship between community and democracy. Dewey argued that democracy is more than a form of government, it is also a mode of associated living. Democratic communities pursue common goals through debate, self-criticism, and exploration. Schools need to be a central force in promoting common ideals, common political institutions, common language, and a common fate that will hold the republic together. Dewey believed that through the unifying ideals of individual freedom, political democracy, and human rights, democracy becomes a mode of interaction among citizens: "The clear consciousness of a communal life, in all its implications, constitutes the idea of democracy."[23]

The pursuit of democratic communities has not been easy in American history. Demographic trends outlined in Chapter 5 indicate the growth of exclusive communities in what can be described as the pursuit of privilege. Under these conditions, it is unclear whether the public and community-building purposes of education will diminish. Educational policy makers at all levels of government set priorities among the core political values of liberty, equality, efficiency, economic growth, and community. They are in strong positions to support the values of democracy and community and the balance of political and social values in American culture.

## Teaching and Learning about Governance

Citizens learn about governance largely through the experience of being governed. Only a small percentage of people become directly involved by participation in a formal decision-making process or by running for political office. However, a majority of Americans attended public schools and experienced governance firsthand within the environment of elementary and secondary education. Teachers and administrators are important models of governance, regardless of their awareness or acceptance of their political roles. One of the troubling ironies within the current system is the authoritarian quality of many school communities. Few educators question that the purpose of schools is to provide an education that is appropriate to a democratic society. Yet many do not make the ethical connection that it is essential to operate schools according to democratic principles.[24] Educators demonstrate varying degrees of democratic or authoritarian control through formal rules, school norms, and interpersonal leadership styles. The culture of a school provides a formative experience in governance for children as well as adults. Educators need to recognize the symbolic implications of school policies ranging from classroom discipline to allocating resources.

Learning the facts about American government and politics is important but less significant than experiencing school and district governance. In order to improve school-level governance, we must reintroduce a broader concept of politics into the educational system. We now teach young people to know about "things." We do not develop the kind of intelligence needed to make public judgments.[25] Research on effective schools shows that teachers and administrators can deal with conflicts in instructive and democratic ways. Effective schools and districts are distinguished by a different kind of conversation, a style of communication that builds community. Although disagreements exist, they are in the open and are the subject of intense and sustained inquiry and debate. Without additional resources, educators have an unlimited number of opportunities to build democratic communities within classrooms and schools. Students can develop critical thinking skills while confronting the never-ending tension between the rights of individuals and the concerns and interests of the larger community.

## Leadership

The job description of administrators centers on managing and controlling school systems. Administrators and policy makers need to prepare for their work in such a way that they recognize the ethical implications of school policies and the responsibility they hold as role models in governance. The demands of political leadership in a democracy are certainly as important as the technical aspects of administration. Donald Schon's model of the "reflective practitioner" is well suited to the preparation of educational administrators. Emphasizing collaboration, the exchange of valid information, commitment to values, and free and open choices, the reflective practitioner is better prepared to deal with the indeterminate, swampy zones of practice that lie beyond the cannons of technical rationality.[26]

Many governance participants will continue to search for solutions to problems without the ability to reframe governance as a process of balancing political values and managing ongoing conflicts. The academic side of educational administration can help prospective school leaders by presenting realistic views of the politics of administration. Higher education faculty and professional associations need to evaluate course offerings and program requirements to determine if they are (1) limited to promoting technical competence, (2) including course work and experiences that prepare people to work in environments that are intellectually, culturally, and politically diverse, and (3) utilizing more democratic and less authoritarian approaches to teaching in order to model the value systems of a democratic society.

As participants in governance, educators find themselves in the middle of four sectors of influential interest groups. They must maintain their position as supporters and educators of democratic values. Representatives from the private sector, from nonprofit groups, and from the media may not accept educators as powerful figures in a community; but as Benjamin Hook argues: "A successful democracy . . . may honor its statesmen; but it must honor its teachers more—whether they be prophets, scientists, poets, jurists, or philosophers. The true hero of democracy, then, should not be the soldier or the political leader, great as their services may be, but the teacher—the Jeffersons, Holmeses, Deweys, Whitmans, and all others who have given the people vision, method, and knowledge."[27]

## Communities and Conversations

Participants in educational governance can begin to converse more effectively and constructively than in the past. In a period of increasing public skepticism about social institutions and a lack of confidence in public education, representatives of public and private organizations can begin to invest more heavily in democratic conversations. William Greider's advice at the end of a gloomy review of American politics is particularly suited to educational administrators and policy makers:

*The simplest, least threatening investment any citizen may make in democratic renewal is to begin talking with other people about important questions. A democratic conversation does not require elaborate rules of procedure or utopian notions of perfect consensus. Those with specialized expertise serve as teachers, not commanders, and will learn themselves from listening to the experience of others. The respect must extend even to hostile adversaries, since the democratic objective is not to destroy them but to reach eventual understanding. At the core, the idea of democracy is as simple as that—a society based on mutual respect.[28]*

Constructive discussions in school board meetings require mutual respect among participants. Administrators cannot control the attitudes and styles of community members, but gradual work that builds on a common language can help bridge the gap between people from differing points of view. Discourse in schools and state legislatures often proceeds with hidden assumptions, different vocabularies, and conflicting metaphors. Without a shared language, different perspectives are likely to produce more contests than collaboration, more gridlock than progress.[29] Changing the culture of governance starts with the use of language, and when people begin to listen to themselves and raise questions about what they hear, they can move from rancorous speeches to real communication.

In order to support a more constructive and democratic governance system, participants at every level of the policy process need to consider both the public and private purposes of education. Administrators and policy makers need political skills to convene and participate in noncoercive, democratic dialogues. Governance conversations, whether at the dinner table or in Congress, can begin to improve if people invest in democracy.

## SEMINAR QUESTIONS

1. Do you think we should move from the current system of governance to a private, market-based system?

2. What can you do as an administrator to improve educational governance?

3. Do you think the value of community should receive higher priority in educational policies?

4. How can you support and improve your community's conversation about education?

## SUGGESTED READINGS

Barber, Benjamin R. *Strong Democracy: Participatory Politics for a New Age.* Berkeley: University of California Press, 1984.

Bellah, Robert N. et al. *The Good Society.* New York: Alfred A. Knopf, 1991.

Greider, William. *Who Will Tell the People?* New York: Touchstone, 1992.

Kozol, Jonothon. *Savage Inequalities.* New York: Crown Publishers, 1991.

Schlesinger, Arthur M. Jr. *The Disuniting of America: Reflections on a Multi-Cultural Society.* New York: W.W. Norton & Co., 1992.

Sergiovanni, Thomas J. and John H. Moore, eds. *Schooling for Tomorrow: Directing Reforms to Issues That Count.* Boston: Allyn & Bacon, 1989.

## ENDNOTES

1. The 26th Annual Phi Delta Kappa/Gallop Poll, Stanley M. Elam, Lowell C. Rose, and Alec M. Gallop, *Phi Delta Kappan* (Washington, DC: Phi Delta Kappa, September 1994).

2. Kenneth A. Sirotnik, "The School as the Center of Change," in *Schooling for Tomorrow: Directing Reforms to Issues That Count,* eds. Thomas J. Sergiovanni and John H. Moore (Boston: Allyn & Bacon, 1989), p. 90.

3. Susan Tifft "National Standards: The Myth—and Danger—of State and Local Control," in *America's Schools and the Mass Media* (New Brunswick, NJ: Transaction Publishers, 1993), pp. 92–93.

4. Henry J. Walberg and Herbert J. Walberg III, "Losing Local Control," *Educational Researcher,* vol. 23, no. 5, (June-July 1994), p. 24.

5. William L. Boyd, "Public Education's Last Hurrah?: Schizophrenia, Amnesia, and Ignorance in School Politics," *Educational Evaluation and Policy Analysis,* vol. 9, no. 2 (Summer 1987), p. 87.

6. Jacqueline P. Danzberger, Michael W. Kirst, and Michael D. Usdan, *Governing Public Schools: New Times, New Requirements* (Washington, DC: Institute for Educational Leadership, 1992), p. 84.

7. Benjamin R. Barber, *Strong Democracy: Participatory Politics for a New Age* (Berkeley: University of California Press, 1984).

8. Larry Cuban, "Reforming Again, Again, and Again," *Educational Researcher* (Washington, DC: American Educational Research Association, January 1990).

9. William L. Boyd, "Public Education's Last Hurrah?: Schizophrenia, Amnesia, and Ignorance in School Politics," *Educational Evaluation and Policy Analysis,* vol. 9, no. 2 (Summer 1987), p. 87.

10. David Osborne and Ted Gaebler, *Reinventing Government* (New York: Plume, 1993), p. 107.

11. Mary Anne Raywid "Choice Orientations, Discussions, and Prospects," *Educational Policy,* vol. 6, no. 2 (June 1992), p. 105–122.

12. Osborne and Gaebler, *Reinventing Government.*

13. Raywid, "Rethinking School Governance," p. 197.

14. Jonothon Kozol, *Savage Inequalities* (New York: Crown Publishers, 1991), p. 62.

15. Myron Lieberman "Lieberman's Law," in *America's Schools and the Mass Media* (New Brunswick, NJ: Transaction Publishers, 1993), p. 6.

16. Joel Spring, *Conflict of Interest: The Politics of American Education* (New York: Longman Publishing Group, 1993).

17. Arthur M. Schlesinger, Jr., *The Disuniting of America* (New York: Longman Publishing Group, 1993).

18. Carl D. Glickman, "Pushing School Reform to a New Edge: The Seven Ironies of School Empowerment." *Phi Delta Kappan* (September, 1990), p. 74.

19. Maenette K. P. Benham and Ronald H. Heck, "Political Culture and Policy in a State-controlled Educational System: The Case of Educational Politics in Hawaii," *Educational Administration Quarterly,* vol. 30, no. 4 (November 1994), p. 419–450.

20. David Tyack, "School Governance in the United States: Historical Puzzles and Anomalies," in *Decentralization and School Improvement,* eds. Jane Hannaway and Martin Carnoy (San Francisco: Jossey-Bass, 1993), p. 25.

21. Robert N. Bellah, et al., *The Good Society* (New York: Alfred A. Knopf, 1991).

22. Joseph Kahne "Democratic Communities, Equity, and Excellence: A Deweyan Reframing of Educational Policy Analysis," *Educational Evaluation and Policy Analysis,* vol. 16, no. 3 (Fall, 1994), p. 233–248.

23. John Dewey, *The Public and its Problems* (Athens, Ohio: Swallow Press, 1927), p. 149.

24. Glickman "Pushing School Reform to a New Edge: The Seven Ironies of School Empowerment," p. 74.

25. Daniel Yankelovich, *Coming to Public Judgment* (Syracuse, New York: Syracuse University Press, 1991), p. 242.

26. Donald A. Schon, *Educating the Reflective Practitioner* (San Francisco: Jossey-Bass, 1987).

27. Sidney Hook, "The Hero and Democracy," *Kettering Review* (Dayton, Ohio: Kettering Foundation, Summer 1993), p. 12.

28. William Greider, *Who Will Tell the People?* (New York: Touchstone, 1992), p. 411.

29. For an explanation of the importance of a common language in school-based reform see, Thomas Bellamy "The Whole School Framework: A Guide for Systemic School-Level Reform," unpublished paper (Denver: University of Colorado at Denver, 1994). Also see Rexford Brown, *Schools of Thought* (San Francisco: Jossey-Bass, 1991).

# INDEX